Celebrate THE Century ™

A COLLECTION OF COMMEMORATIVE STAMPS

1940-1949

CELEBRATE
10
THE CENTURY™
PUT YOUR STAMP
ON HISTORY
1900 ▪ 2000

UNITED STATES
POSTAL SERVICE™

UNITED STATES
POSTAL SERVICE

POSTMASTER GENERAL
AND CHIEF EXECUTIVE OFFICER
William J. Henderson

CHIEF MARKETING OFFICER
Allen Kane

EXECUTIVE DIRECTOR, STAMP SERVICES
Azeezaly S. Jaffer

MANAGER, STAMP MARKETING
Gary A. Thuro

PROJECT MANAGER
Patsy L. Laws

TIME
LIFE
BOOKS

TIME-LIFE BOOKS IS A DIVISION OF TIME LIFE INC.

TIME-LIFE
CUSTOM PUBLISHING

VICE PRESIDENT AND PUBLISHER
Terry Newell

VICE PRESIDENT OF
SALES AND MARKETING
Neil Levin

DIRECTOR OF NEW PRODUCT DEVELOPMENT
Teresa Graham

PRINTING PRODUCTION MANAGER
Carolyn M. Clark

EDITORIAL STAFF FOR
CELEBRATE THE CENTURY

MANAGING EDITOR
Morin Bishop

EDITORS
*John Bolster, Theresa Deal,
Anthony Zumpano*

DESIGNERS
Barbara Chilenskas, Jia Baek

WRITERS
Merrell Noden, Eve Peterson, Rachael Nevins

RESEARCHERS
*Jenny Douglas, Ward Calhoun
Lauren Cardonsky*

PHOTO EDITOR
Bill Broyles

First printing. Printed in U.S.A.

TIME-LIFE is a trademark of Time Warner Inc. U.S.A.

LIBRARY OF CONGRESS CATALOGING-IN-PUBLICATION DATA
Celebrate the century: a collection of commemorative stamps.
p. cm.   Includes index.
Contents: v. 5. 1940–1949
ISBN 0-7835-5321-8
1. Commemorative postage stamps—United States—History—20th century.
2. United States—History—20th century.
I. Time-Life Books

HE6185.U5C45 1998   97–46952
769.56973—DC21   CIP

Books produced by Time-Life Custom Publishing are available at a special bulk discount for promotional and premium use. Custom adaptations can also be created to meet your specific marketing goals. Call 1-800-323-5255.

CONTENTS

America's mobilization after Pearl Harbor (left) led record numbers of women (above) to enter the work force.

INTRODUCTION

The 1940s were to the American people what a phone booth was to Superman—a place of startling transformation. Having just begun to emerge from the shadow of the Great Depression, the United States began the decade in an isolationist frame of mind, with one poll showing that 67 percent of Americans hoped their country would not get involved in the European war. But the United States did enter World War II, and that awful, four-year experience changed the nation utterly, in a variety of unforseen ways. When, in 1941, Henry Luce called this the "American Century," many dismissed the idea as arrogant lunacy. After the war, virtually no American would have disputed it: They took it as an article of faith that their country was the world's leader—economically, militarily and, most significant, morally.

The shift was not so much a real change as a flash of self-recognition: The United States had almost certainly been the richest and most powerful nation on earth for several decades. But the crushing ordeal of the Depression and the long-ingrained habit of regarding Europeans as their cultural superiors meant that most Americans were not ready to acknowledge their nation's puissance. It was almost as if Clark Kent had forgotten what muscles lay hidden beneath that conservative gray suit. World War II changed all that. By the time the war ended with the dropping of atomic bombs on Hiroshima and Nagasaki and the subsequent surrender of the Japanese on August 15, 1945, the United States had begun to put a decidedly American stamp on the world. Many of the international organizations that continue to shape the world today—

the United Nations, the World Bank, and NATO, to name just a few—were the fruit of American leadership in the aftermath of the war.

The country was blessed in its leaders during the '40s, a decade divided almost equally between the administrations of Franklin Delano Roosevelt and Harry S. Truman, two very talented, but very different men. Roosevelt was an independently wealthy, Harvard-educated visionary whose wide-ranging package of New Deal legislation utterly transformed the government's role in the lives of its citizens. Lasting an unprecedented three-and-a-half terms, Roosevelt's tenure epitomized what has come to be known as "the imperial presidency."

Truman, on the other hand, who replaced Henry Wallace as vice president for Roosevelt's final term, was the humble son of Missouri farmers; one sign of Truman's modesty seemed to be the mysterious fact that he had no middle name, just an initial, "S."

The pivotal event of the decade—indeed of the entire century—was World War II, a struggle that soon came to signify a moral Armageddon for both soldiers and civilians. For the first time in history, literally the entire world was embroiled in war. As the long war ground on, month after month, "Remember Pearl Harbor!" became the battle cry of the man in the street, though in truth it was impossible to forget what was going on "over there." Before the war was

Truman proved himself a far more talented leader than many expected.

over, more than 16 million men and women would serve in the U.S. forces, and the U.S. battle toll would come to 292,131 dead and more than 670,000 wounded—roughly the same numbers as in all previous U.S. wars combined.

This was a war Americans experienced viscerally, "the best reported war in history," according to *Time*. From the European front came the steady voice of CBS radio correspondent Edward R. Murrow, whose reports began, "This is London," and often included the screech of air raid sirens and the rumble of bombs exploding. War reportage reached new heights in the writing of Ernie Pyle, whose front line dispatches achieved a kind of grim poetry, and in the cartoons of Bill Mauldin, many of which featured the sardonic pair of unshaven foot soldiers named Willie and Joe.

Meanwhile, back home, extraordinary measures were undertaken as ordinary people were moved by a shared sense of deep purpose. No sacrifice was too great if it contributed to the demise of German dictator Adolf Hitler. Sugar was rationed, then coffee, shoes, canned goods, meat, fats, and cheese. A gasoline curfew went into effect, first in 17 eastern states and then nationwide. President Roosevelt regulated wages, salaries, and prices. Organized labor promised not to strike for the duration of the war. Humming round the clock with a righteous energy, U.S. factories, with a large female work force, cranked out nearly 300,000 military planes during the war.

Swing band leader Glenn Miller, probably the most popular musician of the war years, enlisted and spent the war touring the front lines with his morale-boosting Army Air Force Orchestra. Like many lesser known men, Miller made the ultimate sacrifice when his plane was lost over the English Channel on December 15, 1944.

War fervor had an ugly side too. A kind of paranoia tainted the war effort when in 1942 Roosevelt signed Executive Order 9066, giving the military the power to round up, without warrants or indictments or hearings, all the Japanese-Americans living on the West Coast. Of the 110,000 people who were summarily imprisoned, three quarters were Nisei, children born to Japanese-American parents living in the United States and therefore U.S. citizens themselves. The mass internment was, according to Professor Eugene V. Rostow of Yale Law School, "our worst wartime mistake."

On April 30, 1945, with bombs falling on Berlin, Hitler committed suicide in his bombproof bunker, and a week later the Germans offered a formal surrender. President Truman, who'd taken office just a few weeks earlier, declared May 8 V-E Day. Though it would take nothing less than the spectre of nuclear annihilation to persuade them, the Japanese also surrendered some four months later.

To plan the war's end and its aftermath, the leaders of the three major Allied powers, Roosevelt, English Prime Minister Winston Churchill, and Soviet Premier Josef Stalin had met in February 1945 in the Black Sea resort of Yalta. Perhaps the imminent defeat of Hitler lowered their guards, but Churchill and Roosevelt, those two extraordinarily keen politicians, seem to have completely misread the intentions of "Uncle Joe," as Roosevelt called him. Even

The GI Bill made a college education possible for millions of returning veterans.

Truman, normally the most clear-eyed of men, returned from a summit at Potsdam saying, "I like Uncle Joe."

But the avuncular butcher of some 20 million of his countrymen had never given up his original aim of revolutionizing the world and very quickly installed puppet governments in all the countries on Russia's western border. Roosevelt died just two months after Yalta, but Churchill lived to recognize his misjudgment. In March, 1946, barely a year after he and Roosevelt had sat down with Stalin in Yalta, he made his grim pronouncement: "From Stettin in the Baltic to Trieste in the Adriatic an iron curtain has descended across the Continent."

Tensions between the United States and its former World War II ally would color all foreign policy for the next 30 years. It also made for tremendous paranoia back home. In 1947 Truman set up "loyalty boards" to keep tabs on federal employees, particularly those suspected of being so-called Communist sympathizers. The following year Whittaker Chambers made headlines when he accused Alger Hiss, the liberal president of the Carnegie Endowment for International Peace, of being a Communist. Hiss denied the allegations, but was convicted of perjury in a sensational trial. The case still stirs passionate debate.

What it means to be an American seems always to be changing—perhaps more dramatically in the 1940s than in any other decade, when World War II acted as a kind of crucible for the creation of the American middle class, with the GI Bill as its flame. By guaranteeing a college education to every veteran who had been honorably discharged, the GI Bill, signed into law on June 22, 1944, placed higher education within the grasp of ordinary Americans, raising their expectations and increasing their stake in the country's success.

The war also transformed the attitudes of African-Americans, more than one million of whom, after serving in mostly segregated forces, came home determined to fight for rights they'd been promised but not given. They could look to two great sports champions of the 1940s for inspi-

A new generation helped drive the economy to dizzying heights.

ration. One was "the Brown Bomber," boxer Joe Louis, who held the heavyweight title longer than any man to this day (11 years, 9 months), successfully defending it 25 times. In 1947 Jackie Robinson integrated the national game of baseball at its highest level, winning the rookie of the year award for Branch Rickey's Brooklyn Dodgers.

Women, too, having served their country both overseas and at home, saw themselves in a new light. Not only did the number of women in the work force jump 50 percent during the war, from 12 to 18 million, but the women who were already working were now paid better and given more responsibility.

Even teenagers became an economic and cultural force. With money in their pockets and austerity measures lifted, young people were dating again. Two thousand drive-in movie theaters opened between 1947 and 1950. By 1946 the revived record industry was selling 10 times the number of records it had 10 years earlier. Many of those records wound up in jukeboxes, which gobbled an astonishing five billion nickels a year. Young people danced the Lindy Hop, or Jitterbug, to swing bands led by "cats" like Benny Goodman, Count Basie, Cab Calloway, and Duke Ellington. They flocked to dance palaces like the Savoy in Harlem and Roseland in midtown Manhattan, where they competed in acrobatic dance contests. Almost overnight, Frank Sinatra went from cult singer to "The Voice," after one swoon-inducing concert at the Paramount Theater in New York City.

Not all the art being produced in the 1940s was as upbeat as swing. A number of writers openly questioned the American dream. In 1940 Orson Welles made his first film, *Citizen Kane,* which is still considered by many to be the finest American film ever made. Playwright Tennessee Williams scored a huge Broadway hit with *A Street-car Named Desire,* which introduced handsome, muscular Marlon Brando to the world. And a year later Arthur Miller gave us *Death of a Salesman,* the story of Willy Loman, the exhausted traveling salesman whose life had once seemed so much bigger.

At the same time, New York was replacing Paris as the epicenter of the visual arts. The American movement known as Abstract Expressionism, led by artists such as Willem de Kooning, Mark Rothko, and Jackson Pollock, grew in influence. What appeared on the canvas—most famously Jackson Pollock's "drip" paintings—was said to be the unedited chaos of the id.

And bringing all of these startling changes home to ordinary Americans was the television. In 1945 the television was a slightly distrusted luxury that resided in just 8,000 American homes. By January 1950, three million television sets were in use, tuning in to favorites like Milton Berle, "Mr. Television," or his rival, Ed Sullivan.

It would be hard now to pin down what precisely defines our modern world at the end of the "American Century." Is it the awareness of our capacity for nuclear annihilation? Or is it "ethnic cleansing," which is not unique to this century but which certainly attained a new level of ghoulishness with Adolf Hitler? Perhaps it's

Jackie Robinson's destruction of baseball's color barrier earned him the admiration of both black and white fans.

nothing as tragic or grim as either of those, but something more hopeful, the promise of a single world community linked by modern technology. However we might now characterize what it means to be citizens of the world in the late twentieth century, that meaning was shaped mightily in the 1940s, ten years of startling change for America and the world.

BABY BOOM

Demographers expected only a fleeting rise in childbearing following World War II. After all, fertility rates had long been declining in the United States. Americans were too busy having fun in the 1920s to think about raising families, and the bleak Depression years of the '30s produced a paltry batch of babies. But returning GIs and their long-suffering war brides and sweethearts had something else altogether in mind, and it resulted in a boom that would echo well into the twenty-first century.

Not that there hadn't been signs of what was to come. Swept up in a sort of desperate and patriotic romanticism, American soldiers and girls hastily tied the knot before parting for what might be eternity. The unattached searched for and frequently found mates at the country's more than 3,000 USO centers—converted churches, clubs, museums and even railroad cars where coffee and doughnuts were plentiful but dating was officially proscribed. "Furlough babies" goosed the birth rate as early as 1942.

Life on the front, however, was far from romantic. Uniformed men, extremely well supplied in most areas, made up for the lack of "dames" by papering their walls, helmets and lockers with photos of Rita Hayworth, Betty Grable and *Esquire* magazine's monthly pinup girls. "Sugar reports" from home were eagerly awaited in the mails but ultimately must have added to frustrated feelings of desire and expectation. On the homefront women read censored missives from their loved ones, pitched in to the war effort by doing everything from factory work to donating nylon stockings, and waited.

When it came, V-J Day signaled not only the end of war, but also the beginning of national renewal à la Ozzie and Harriet. The country could believe in peace, prosperity and the American

Crowded schools (left), toddler races (above), and a host of other kid-related phenomena typified the Baby Boom.

The Saturday Evening Post illustration ©The Curtis Publishing Company.

dream—a dream centered on home, the nuclear family, car ownership and, ultimately, an even better life for the next generation. In 1946 the marriage rate catapulted 42 percent to a record 2.2 million unions. Men and women were eager to at last begin a family after suffering a decade and a half of privations borne of the economic depression and war. They had served their country, and now their country would help them resume, even celebrate, their lives. Even those who had been too young to be marked by the Depression felt buoyed by the robust economy and wide-open job market. They married younger and had babies sooner.

In May 1946, nine months after V-J Day, birth rates rose; in June they rose again; by October they had reached record levels. As one historian put it, "the cry of the baby was heard across the land." That year 3.4 million babies were born, a 20 percent rise from the year before. And the boom had just begun. The annual number of newborns would hit the four million mark for 10

years running beginning in 1954. All told, the 20-year span from 1946 to 1964 produced 76.4 million births.

There was, however, one caveat. Wartime priorities had imposed a moratorium on homebuilding and by the end of 1945 some 1.25 million GIs per month were returning only to find themselves homeless. Families doubled up; they camped in military barracks and even cars. With jobs aplenty, babies everywhere, and cars rolling off assembly lines once again, the stage was set for the mass

"The baby boom...was perhaps the most amazing social trend of the postwar era."

—*JAMES T. PATTERSON,* *author of* **Grand Expectations**

When servicemen (right) returned home to their rapidly expanding families (above), many, like the naval officers on the opposite page, were forced to share apartments with one another.

exodus to suburbia that would forever change the face of urban America.

Nobody understood the appeal of a patch of grass and two bedrooms better than William J. Levitt, who, during a few short months in 1947, converted 6,000 acres of Long Island potato fields into a prefab commuter community named Levittown that housed 80,000 residents in 17,000 homes. The basic model cost $7,990. And with the help of generous government loans, the working class, or at least the white working class, eagerly bought a slice of America's suburban dream.

A New York pediatrician with an interest in psychology helped nurture that dream. Dr. Benjamin Spock's *The Common Sense Book of Baby and Child Care*, published in 1945, quickly became the child-rearing bible for hundreds of thousands of new parents. Spock was convinced that mothers should stay home to care for their newborns and toddlers, a notion that dovetailed neatly into emerging social trends. Indeed, 86 percent of America's mothers remained at home with their baby boomers, who by 1964 accounted for nearly two-fifths of the country's population.

Aftermath

By 1957, the height of the baby boom, a baby was born in this country every seven seconds for a total of 12,343 new Americans per day. With a current rate of one birth every eight seconds, or 10,800 per day, 563,095 fewer babies are born annually. At the same time, more mothers have taken to the workplace: As of 1997, 71.9 percent of the nation's mothers were part of the labor force. Still, with baby boomers moving toward retirement, employers will soon be facing a long-term labor shortage. It is estimated that by 2020, the 55-and-older segment of Americans will have risen by 73 percent while the prime work-force age group will have grown by only 5 percent. This unprecedented demographic shift has provoked grave concern for the solvency of the nation's social security system.

With the baby boom in full swing and kids flooding schoolyards (top) and playgrounds (opposite page) all across the country, massive suburban developments like Levittown (above), on New York's Long Island, provided the affordable housing America's newest families desperately needed.

A STREETCAR NAMED DESIRE

When he explained why he decided to change his first name, playwright Tennessee Williams pointed out that his given name, Thomas Lanier Williams, sounded "like it might belong to the sort of writer who turns out sonnet sequences to spring." Tennessee Williams did write poetry, but is rightly best known for the lyricism of such plays as *The Glass Menagerie* (1945) and *A Streetcar Named Desire* (1947), which won the hearts of audiences and critics alike and secured his place among America's greatest dramatists.

From his birth on March 26, 1911, through the first seven years of his life, Williams and his older sister, Rose, lived with their mother and her parents in the Episcopalian rectories of various towns in Mississippi where their grandfather was a minister. In the summer of 1918, Williams's father, who traveled selling men's shoes and clothing, landed a managerial position

with the International Shoe Company and moved the family to St. Louis. The transition from genteel small-town life with their grandparents to the family's cramped, dark quarters in St. Louis shocked young Tom and Rose, especially as relations between their Southern-belle mother and hard-drinking father exploded in unconcealed hostility.

Williams's literary efforts began in the early 1920s, when his mother bought him a used portable typewriter in the hopes that it might help him with his junior high-school assignments. "It immediately became my place of retreat, my cave, my refuge," he later wrote of the escape the typewriter provided from his unhappy home life.

While Williams escaped into the worlds he conjured up on his typewriter, his sister withdrew from the tensions at home into the fantasies of schizophrenic delusion. In his first critical and

Streetcar's original Broadway production (above) featured a smoldering Marlon Brando and a fragile Jessica Tandy (left).

17

The Kowalskis' tiny apartment could barely contain all the life within it, which included poker games (above) and birthday celebrations (top), not to mention Stanley's explosive sexuality (right); the spatial limitations lent Williams's play a powerful sense of cramped longing and pent-up violence.

popular hit, *The Glass Menagerie*, produced in 1945, Williams transformed the anguish he felt for his sister into what reviewer Ashton Stevens called "true poetry couched in colloquial prose."

This hit also altered Williams's real life; suddenly transported to a first-class hotel in Manhattan after a "life of clawing and scratching along a sheer surface and holding on tight with raw fin-

gers to every inch of rock higher than the one caught hold of before," he confronted what he later termed "the catastrophe of Success"—the "catastrophe" being, he said, "the vacuity of a life without struggle."

As always, he found meaning and refuge in his writing. In the summer of '45 he took off for Mexico, where he began developing a collection

Streetcar, written by Williams (far right) and produced by Irene Selznik (near right), went on to win a Pulitzer Prize and become a successful film, with Brando, Kim Hunter and Karl Malden all reprising their stage roles.

of scenes into what he then called *The Poker Night*. More than a year later, in New Orleans, those scenes began to take narrative and thematic shape. Williams found one of the play's symbols rattling back and forth on the road just outside his home in the French Quarter. "Down this street, running on the same tracks, are two streetcars, one named 'Desire' and the other named

"**He wanted not to approve or disapprove but to touch the germ of life and to celebrate it with verbal beauty.**"

—*ARTHUR MILLER on Tennessee Williams, March 1984*

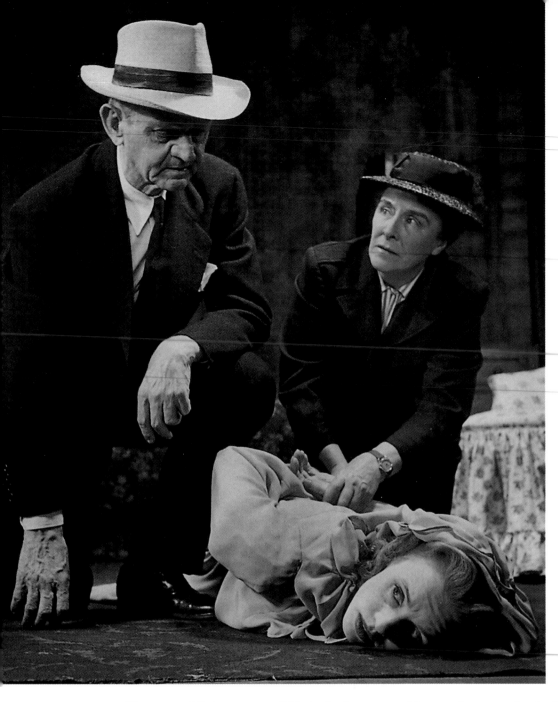

family's estate and come to New Orleans to stay with her younger sister, Stella, in the two-room flat Stella shares with her husband, Stanley Kowalski. Upon hearing about the lost estate, Stanley at once searches through Blanche's suitcase and finds beads and rhinestones, which he mistakes for pearls and diamonds. "I have an acquaintance that works in a jewelry store. I'll have him in here to make an appraisal of this," he says. In his appraisal of Blanche's past, Stanley eventually finds that much more than her jewelry is sham and cruelly exposes her, denying her a last hope for happiness.

The play's December 3, 1947, New York premiere brought the audience to its feet for a full half-hour of applause. British actress Jessica Tandy and a 23-year-old Marlon Brando, both virtual unknowns, had given full

'Cemetery,' " he wrote. "Their indiscourageable progress up and down Royal [Street] struck me as having some symbolic bearing of a broad nature on the life in the Vieux Carré—and everywhere else for that matter."

For the play, Williams altered the actual streetcar route so that his heroine can, as she says in her first line, "take a streetcar named Desire, and then transfer to one called Cemeteries and ride six blocks and get off at—Elysian Fields!" Blanche DuBois has lost what remained of her

and sympathetic life to the erotically charged clash between the brute realist who fought and survived World War II and the feeble idealist who longs for magic but can effect only the illusion of it. "I don't tell truth, I tell what ought to be true," says Blanche. "Never inside, I didn't lie in my heart." Through the figure of Blanche DuBois, Tennessee Williams mourned the lives of America's lost and unhappy romantics, forced to live in a land that had never been as innocent as it seemed.

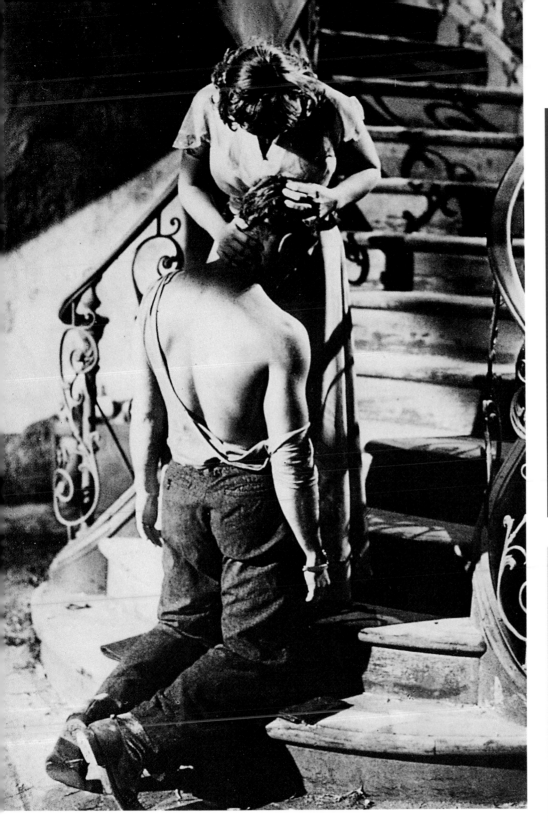

Aftermath

Vivien Leigh (as Blanche), Karl Malden (Mitch) and Kim Hunter (Stella) won Oscars for their work in the 1951 film adaptation of *Streetcar*. After more than half a century the play remains a popular choice for both professional and amateur productions. The most recent Broadway revival, in 1992, starred Jessica Lange and Alec Baldwin.

Until his death in 1983, Williams continued to write plays with increasingly dark and difficult sexual themes, including such hits as *Cat on a Hot Tin Roof* and *Suddenly Last Summer*.

In the play's harrowing final scene, a traumatized Blanche (opposite page) is examined and then taken away to a mental institution. Perhaps the most famous scene in the filmed version has Brando (right) as a repentant Stanley howling Stella's name outside their neighbor's apartment until she emerges and forgives him (above) for his violence toward her.

JACKIE ROBINSON

After helping vanquish the Axis powers during World War II, many black soldiers returned to the United States to face another enemy: Jim Crow. Although the Civil Rights Act of 1866 established blacks as American citizens and forbade discrimination against them, segregation laws caused them to be anything but equal to whites in most aspects of American life.

Major League Baseball™ was no exception. Despite the proven abilities of such black stars as Satchel Paige, James "Cool Papa" Bell and Josh Gibson, they and other African-American ballplayers were banished to The Negro Leagues™, which were popular but not as organized and successful as "white" baseball. The color line seemed uncrossable.

Branch Rickey, president of the Brooklyn Dodgers™, carefully—and secretly—sought to change that. In 1945 he created a new circuit, the United States League, to compete with the Negro Leagues, which he decried as "rackets" for their lack of standard contracts and regular schedules. Collapsing after only one season, the league may well have been a smoke screen that allowed Rickey to scout black players for promotion to the Major Leagues without causing suspicion.

Several players were recommended, but based on a combination of baseball ability and personal history, Rickey pinned his hopes on Jackie Robinson, the shortstop of the Kansas City Monarchs™. Robinson was already well known from his years at UCLA where he excelled in football, basketball, track and baseball to become the university's first four-letter man.

By the time Robinson re-signed with Rickey (top, right) in 1950, his days in a Montreal uniform (left) were a fond memory.

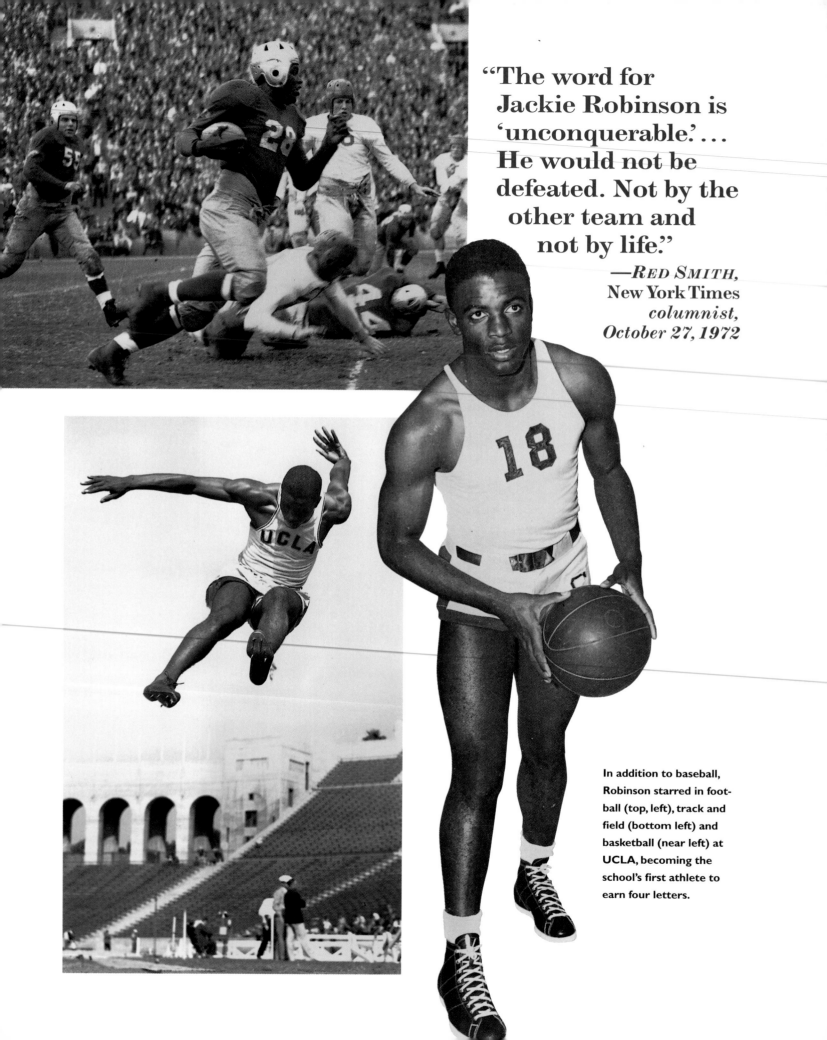

"The word for
Jackie Robinson is
'unconquerable.'...
He would not be
defeated. Not by the
other team and
not by life."
—*RED SMITH,*
New York Times
columnist,
October 27, 1972

In addition to baseball,
Robinson starred in foot-
ball (top, left), track and
field (bottom left) and
basketball (near left) at
UCLA, becoming the
school's first athlete to
earn four letters.

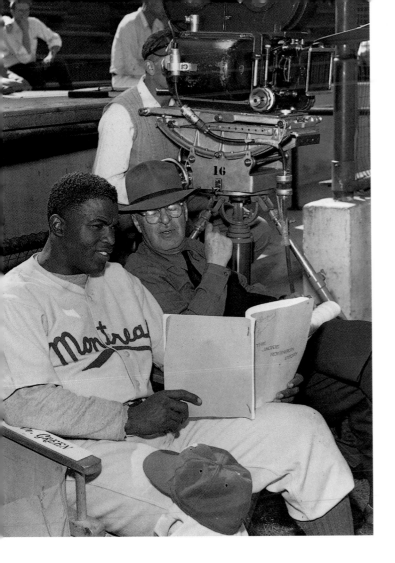

Robinson (above with wife Rachel in 1949) was always willing to get politically involved when he thought he could help; in 1950 the now popular Robinson (left, with director Al Green) starred in the movie treatment of his life.

What impressed Rickey most, though, was Robinson's character. In 1944, as an army lieutenant, Robinson faced a court-martial for insubordination: He had argued with military police and a base provost marshal for siding with a bus driver who, despite the army's policy of desegregation on military buses, ordered Robinson "to the back of the bus where the colored people belonged." The army ruled that Robinson had acted within his rights in refusing to change seats.

On August 28, 1945, Robinson and Rickey had their historic first encounter in Brooklyn. Playing the part of racist fans, spiteful teammates and vengeful opponents, the executive demonstrated the insults and abuses that Robinson would likely suffer if he penetrated the all-white league. "Mr. Rickey," Robinson finally asked, "do you want a ballplayer who's afraid to fight back?"

"I want a player with guts enough not to fight back," Rickey replied, fearing that any outburst by Robinson, however justified, could set back baseball integration for several years. In the end, Rickey chose Robinson not because he was the most talented black player available, but because he believed Robinson possessed the courage and the stamina needed to survive the virulent racism his presence would inevitably provoke. Simply stated, Rickey believed that Robinson would stick it out.

Robinson joined the Montreal Royals™, the Dodgers Minor League team in the International League, in 1946. He led the league in batting with a .349 average, a performance that helped persuade Rickey that he was ready to make the move to the major leagues the following season. On Tuesday, April 15, 1947, Opening Day, Robinson

made his debut at Ebbets Field against the Boston Braves™. He went hitless, reaching first base once on an error, but the next day he got the first of his 1,518 career hits, a bunt single off Glenn Elliott.

In the games that followed, Rickey's predictions of prejudice proved accurate. Many fans jeered Robinson. Opposing players hurled racial slurs from the dugout. Pitchers tried to bean him, opponents attempted to spike him—even death threats were not uncommon. Some of his own teammates circulated a petition to keep him off the Dodgers. But throughout his rookie season, Robinson turned the other cheek, as Rickey had advised, winning over thousands of fans and most of his teammates in the process.

Despite these and other hardships—Jim Crow laws barred Robinson from many hotels and restaurants used by his teammates on road trips—the 28-year-old batted .297 and was named Rookie of the Year. Two years later he had an MVP season, leading the league in batting (.342) and stolen bases (37) while helping the Dodgers to the pennant.

Robinson opened the door for other blacks to follow him into the major leagues: Larry Doby signed with the Cleveland Indians™ on July 3, 1947, to become the first black player in the American League™, and Robinson's teammates soon included former Negro Leaguers Roy Campanella and Don Newcombe. By 1951, 14 blacks were in the majors and all but three teams had a black player under contract somewhere in their major- or minor-league systems.

That year five of the 14 black players, including Jackie Robinson, were elected to the All-Star team, and with full integration soon to follow, Rickey's "great experiment" was an unqualified success.

Aftermath

Robinson ended his 10-year career with a .311 batting average and six All-Star and World Series™ appearances, including a world championship in 1955. He was elected to the Baseball Hall of Fame™ in 1962, his first year on the ballot.

Robinson remained a public figure after baseball as a commercial pitchman, vice president of Chock Full O' Nuts, and political and civil rights activist. He frequently criticized baseball for its lack of black managers and executives.

Suffering from heart disease and diabetes, Robinson passed away at age 53 on October 24, 1972. His death came just nine days after Robinson threw out the first pitch of Game 2 of the Oakland-Cincinnati World Series while being honored for his historic entry into the Major Leagues 25 years earlier.

Throughout the 1997 season, baseball celebrated the 50th anniversary of Jackie Robinson's rookie year. On April 15, in an unprecedented tribute, Robinson's Dodgers jersey number (42) was simultaneously retired by every major-league team.

Robinson's daring on the base paths (opposite page, top) produced 19 steals of home; Robinson's 1950 baseball card (opposite page) now listed an MVP season on its back; Leo Durocher (above) was Robinson's first major-league manager; by 1949, Robinson's teammates included Campanella and Newcombe (top, to Robinson's right and left respectively); Robinson's trip to the '49 All-Star Game™ saw him teamed with (top right, left to right) Stan Musial, Gil Hodges and Ralph Kiner.

HARRY S. TRUMAN

When Harry Truman succeeded President Franklin D. Roosevelt, who died in office on April 12, 1945, Americans were nervous—none more so, in fact, than the new president. "I felt like the moon, the stars, and all the planets had fallen on me," said Truman, who inherited several issues—including the development of the atomic bomb and looming difficulties with Russia—about which he had been kept in the dark as vice president.

Truman seemed to shrink in the shadow of the towering FDR, who led the country through the Depression and most of World War II. Unlike the patrician Roosevelt, Truman was a one-time farmer who failed in nearly every business venture he tried, from oil drilling to haberdashery. As a two-term U.S. Senator from Missouri who chaired a committee investigating the abuse of government defense contracts, Truman was respected, but his connections to the Kansas City political machine still dogged him. He was a poor speaker and not as well educated as Roosevelt. Not surprisingly, there weren't many who had high hopes for Truman's presidency. Even Truman admitted that there may be "a million" men more qualified to be president.

The war in Europe was winding down as Truman took office. Victory in Europe was celebrated on May 8, 1945, Truman's 61st birthday, and on July 2 the new president urged the Senate to ratify the United Nations Charter to end the isolationism that had prevented the country from joining the League of Nations after World War I.

Meanwhile, the war continued to rage in the Pacific. Though weakened by nearly nonstop bombings of its cities, Japan would not surrender. An invasion of the country would be long and bloody; based on the likely fierce resistance of the Japanese army, estimates of American casualties in such an attack ran from 220,000 to one million.

So when Secretary of War Henry L. Stimson

Truman's popular whistle-stop tour (above) helped him disprove predictions of election defeat (left).

Prior to becoming a United States senator, Truman (inset) had served as a captain in World War I (right, second row, third from right) and been co-proprietor of a failed men's clothing shop in Kansas City, Missouri (above).

informed Truman of the Manhattan Project—the secret, $2 billion operation that produced the world's first atomic bomb—the president saw another option. He hoped the bomb's swift destruction of its target would "shock" the Japanese into surrender. When "Fat Man" was dropped over Hiroshima on August 6, 1945, it killed an estimated 60,000 people, mostly civilians, instantly. But Japan made no response. Truman ordered a second bomb, "Little Boy," to be dropped on Nagasaki on August 9, resulting in another 80,000 Japanese casualties, and followed it with a 1,000-plane air raid on Tokyo. Japan finally surrendered on the evening of August 14.

Truman's decision to use the atomic bomb—and particularly his bombing of Nagasaki—has engendered much controversy, with some critics arguing that a Japanese surrender could have been engineered without such horrifying loss of human life. Some have even suggested, with very limited evidence, that Truman dropped the atomic bomb primarily to send a message of American military strength to Russia. When all is said and done, no decision more fully illustrated the painful character of the now familiar maxim that Truman popularized: The buck stops here.

Victory in World War II did not end trouble abroad. The Axis powers were crushed, but Communism soon emerged as the new world menace.

"America has faith in people. It knows that leaders rise and fall, but that the people live on."

—HARRY TRUMAN, June 16, 1948

Accompanied by his wife Bess and daughter Margaret (above, middle and right, respectively), Truman returned from Independence, Missouri, to Washington to brief president-elect Dwight Eisenhower on the nation's problems.

Several Eastern European countries fell under the control of the Soviet Union, and when Greece and Turkey were threatened in 1947, Truman appealed to Congress for aid to those nations under a program later called the Truman Doctrine.

Looking to prevent another postwar depression and the politically unstable conditions that would accompany it, Congress approved the administration's European Recovery Program—informally known as the Marshall Plan for Secretary of State George Marshall—to stimulate the war-ravaged economy in Western Europe.

While the Marshall Plan was being approved, the Soviet Union blockaded land routes to Berlin in response to the Allies' introduction of a new currency meant to economically unify their occupation zones. Declaring "We would stay, period," Truman chose to not break the blockade, but instead launched a massive airlift to bring food and supplies to the city. When the blockade ended after 14 months, 277,804 flights had moved 2,325,809 tons of food and supplies into Berlin.

In spite of his forceful response to these challenges, Truman was considered an underdog in the 1948 election against Thomas Dewey, the Republican governor of New York. The October 11, 1948, issue of *Newsweek* trumpeted the magazine's poll of 50 top political writers that

Truman's affable nature brings smiles to journalists (above) and world leaders like Winston Churchill and Joseph Stalin (left, at the Potsdam Conference).

predicted the outcome: Dewey 50, Truman 0.

But Truman's relentless "Whistle-stop Campaign," during which he traveled 21,928 miles in 33 days by rail, accentuated his folksy appeal and resulted in an election day outcome that surprised nearly everyone except Truman himself. He was reelected with 303 electoral votes to Dewey's 189 and by a slim margin of 2,100,000 popular votes.

The next day Truman's train to Washington stopped briefly in St. Louis, where someone handed the president an election-night edition of the *Chicago Tribune*. Photographers captured a beaming Truman holding the paper aloft in what became one of the most famous photos in Ameri-

can politics. The paper's not-so-prophetic headline read: DEWEY DEFEATS TRUMAN.

Though Truman was unpopular for most of his presidency—many called him "that little man," more for his stature than his height—historians have been much kinder. He is often ranked among the top eight presidents in history for his character, his progressive domestic policies, and his efforts in shaping a postwar world faced with Communism. In the words of Pulitzer Prize-winning biographer David McCullough, "As much as any president since Lincoln, he brought to the highest office the language and values of the common American people.... He *was* America."

A worried Truman made his first national radio address five days after taking office (above); the nation would come to admire Truman's plain-spoken quality, summed up in the sign "The Buck Stops Here!" that sat on his Oval Office desk (top, right).

Aftermath

The '50s brought little respite to Truman's presidency. Threat of another world war arose on June 24, 1950, when Soviet-backed North Koreans invaded South Korea. American troops joined United Nations forces in the conflict while Truman made several difficult decisions—including a refusal to use nuclear weapons and the firing of the popular General Douglas MacArthur for disobeying his orders. In 1953 the "police action" ended—indecisively to some, but to Truman it signaled a victory over military aggression.

Despite being exempt from the 1951 constitutional amendment restricting the presidency to two terms, Truman chose not to run for reelection in 1952.

He spent his remaining years in his hometown of Independence, Missouri, and died on December 26, 1972, at age 88.

INTERNATIONAL STYLE

Ludwig Mies van der Rohe, Walter Gropius, Le Corbusier, J.J.P. Oud—these were the brilliant young architects of post–World War I Germany, France and Holland. That their socialist visions of Utopian cities for the masses and inexpensive workers' housing would in two short decades pave the way for the modern American corporate icon— the steel and glass skyscraper— exemplifies the long, strange road that history often follows.

An expression of the age of mass production, the architecture of Mies, Gropius, Le Corbusier and Oud eschewed excessive ornamentation in favor of a restrained, user-oriented vocabulary featuring crisp, spare surfaces, simple geometric forms, strip windows and flat roofs. But if these pioneers rejected nearly all historical antecedents, they nonetheless adhered to classical ideals of proportion and simplicity. Rather than hewing marble or stone, they built with prefabricated steel and concrete.

Although the individual practitioners of what would later be called International Style drew from influences as varied as futurism, American industrial design, Frank Lloyd Wright's organic architecture and the de Stijl art movement of Mondrian, van Doesburg, and Rietveld, their work shared a common ideal: that architecture should serve humanity and should embody its economic and social context. Open floor plans allowed for greater flexibility in use, especially for residences. Machine-age details connected users to their era of rapid industrialization. And standardized design elements made for ease and economy in construction.

Examples of this new architecture were unveiled in the United States at the critically acclaimed 1932 Museum of Modern Art exhibition. But the show's curators, Henry-Russell Hitchcock and Philip Johnson, chose not to dwell on the social context and content of what they

Johnson's Glass House (above) was a high point of the style, but the U.N. building (left) inspired a wave of cheap knockoffs.

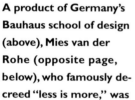

A product of Germany's Bauhaus school of design (above), Mies van der Rohe (opposite page, below), who famously decreed "less is more," was a leading proponent of the International Style, favoring open, "universal spaces" in his design (opposite page, above) for the IIT campus (right).

dubbed International Style. Instead they focused on its guiding aesthetic principles: 1) an emphasis on "volume" (interior space) as opposed to "mass" (structural bulk), 2) organization around regularity rather than symmetry or obvious balance, and 3) the avoidance of decoration.

The show included works by American architects Hood, Howe & Lescaze, Austrian-born Neutra, and, by way of contrast, Frank Lloyd Wright. But the movement only gained momentum in the United States once Mies and Gropius emigrated in the late '30s after fleeing Nazi Germany.

The two practiced and preached their highly developed vernacular from their respective posi-

tions at the Illinois Institute of Technology (IIT) and Harvard University schools of architecture. Mies quickly set to work designing the IIT campus (1939 to 1941) using exposed structural steel and large sheets of glass to enclose essentially open interior spaces. While his famous dictum "less is more" was perhaps best exemplified in the pure and weightless forms of the Farnsworth House (1948 to 1950), the project that broke ground for the flood of spare, steel-and-glass skyscrapers that characterized U.S. architecture from the post–World War II years through the mid-'70s was The Lake Shore Drive Apartments (1949 to 1951). As architect Helmut Jahn has opined, "I

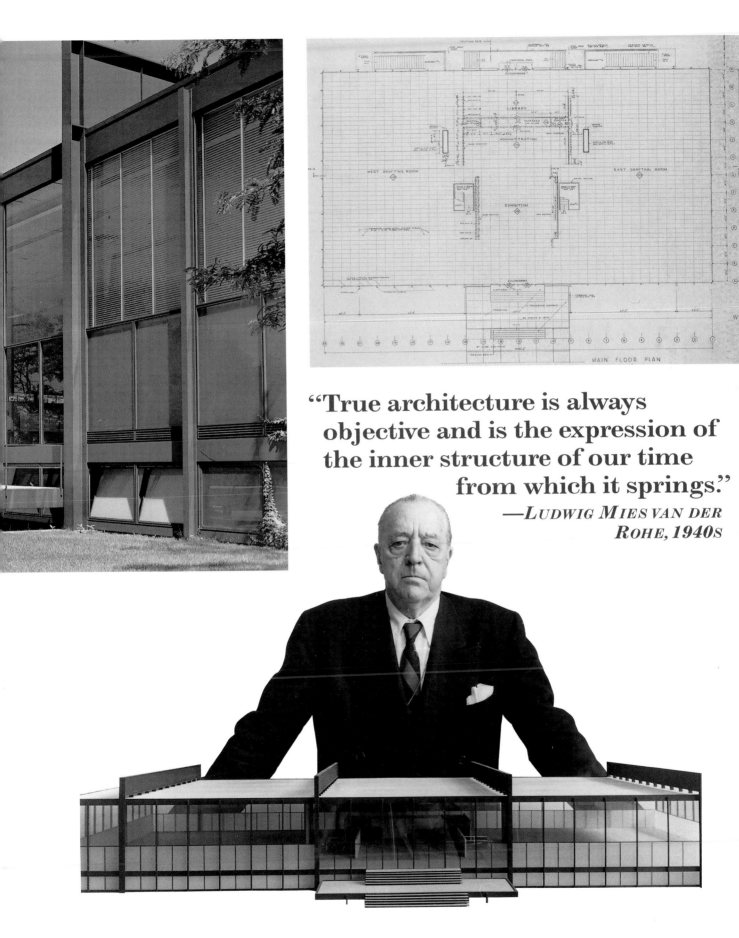

MAIN FLOOR PLAN

"True architecture is always
objective and is the expression of
the inner structure of our time
from which it springs."
—*Ludwig Mies van der
Rohe, 1940s*

dare even to say that architecture would be different today if 860–880 Lake Shore Drive had not been built."

Despite many outstanding examples of International Style in the United States, among them Richard Neutra's Kaufmann Desert House in Palm Springs (1946 to 1947) and Johnson's Glass House in New Canaan, Connecticut, most architectural historians feel that something important of the original idiom got lost either during World War II or in the American translation, or both. Take the Le Corbusier-inspired U.N. Secretariat building (1947 to 1950). It was New York's first glass-curtain-walled skyscraper, and it heralded the arrival of lightness and airiness in a city of dense, closed spaces. With in less than a decade, cheap knockoffs proliferated. As with the workers' housing designed in post–World War I Europe, these gleaming glass and steel buildings— paeans to corporate culture—were signs of their time.

As Johnson himself, once the chief propagandist of International Style, wrote in 1995, "The International Style had a longer life, it seems to me now, than it ever deserved." Yet in the same paragraph, he says of the 1932 exhibition he co-curated, "[It] established architecture in the art world's eyes. It made architecture a respectable endeavor."

The radiant interior of Johnson's Glass House (opposite page, above), its "podium"-mounted exterior (opposite page, below), Neutra's Palm Springs' Kaufmann

Desert House (top), Mies's Farnsworth House (inset) and The Lake Shore Drive Apartments (above, right) are International touchstones.

Aftermath

Architect Robert Venturi wrote, "Less is a bore" in his 1966 book *Complexity and Contradiction in Architecture.* He seemed to echo the sentiments of many Americans who, by the late '70s, happily joined the movement that came to be known as post-Modernism. Even Johnson, who had grown tired of the glass box, defected to more decorative styles.

WORLD WAR II

The notion of World War I as the "war to end all wars" was sadly and terribly debunked with the outbreak of World War II, the most epic conflict in history and the pivotal event of the twentieth century. Truly a global war, its battles raged from New Guinea to Norway, from Tokyo to Tripoli, and nothing less than the fate of the free world depended on its outcome.

The loss of human life was staggering. By war's end, more than 15,000,000 were dead, including 405,000 from the United States and a stunning 6,115,000 from the Soviet Union, the nation most severely brutalized by the conflict. Only later did the world learn of the war's most horrifying cruelty: the death of more than 6,000,000 people—men, women, and children—in Adolf Hitler's death camps.

The hostilities, which had simmered for most of the 1930s, boiled over in 1939 when German chancellor Hitler invaded Poland. Great Britain and France immediately declared war against Germany. By 1941 Japan, an increasingly aggressive force in Asia, and Italy, the fascist invader of North Africa, had joined Germany to form the Axis alliance, and France had fallen to Hitler.

For two years the United States's participation in the war was limited to supplying arms to the Allies while attempting diplomatically to contain Japan in the Pacific. That changed in the early morning hours of December 7, 1941, when 353 Japanese fighter planes and bombers materialized in the haze above Pearl Harbor, Hawaii, where the U.S. Navy's Pacific Fleet was stationed. The sneak attack killed more than 2,400 Americans and cut the navy in half.

British prime minister Winston Churchill called Pearl Harbor one of the "grand climacterics" of World War II because of the effect it had on America. The country's massive capability for production was already mobilized in support of the Allies, and

Japan's devastating attack on Pearl Harbor (above) sent hundreds of thousands of Americans off to war (left).

41

now, galvanized by Pearl Harbor, it kicked into high gear. The draft had been reinstituted in 1940 and the U.S. armed forces counted 1.5 million trained soldiers and officers. Never in its history had the country been more prepared for war.

Despite a general call for revenge against Japan, President Franklin Roosevelt stuck to the Allied strategy of defeating Germany first. The tactic rested on the belief that Japan could wait, but Germany—which was close to toppling Russia and Britain to control all of Europe—could not. If Germany were defeated, then Russia and Britain could join the United States in vanquishing Japan.

Thus after establishing a containing force in the Pacific, the United States turned its attention to Europe. In late 1942 the Allies made a combined assault on North Africa and the Axis forces there. Their success was, as Churchill put it, "the end of

the beginning" and allowed the Allies entry to Europe through its "soft underbelly," Italy.

Even while launching the Italian campaign and beefing up its Pacific force, the United States cooperated with the Allies in a massive invasion of Europe from the West. The greatest amphibious assault ever launched, the operation set forth on June 6, 1944—D-Day. Some 175,000 American, British and Canadian soldiers stormed five beaches on France's Normandy coast and caught the Germans, who had anticipated an invasion farther north, somewhat off guard. Still, the Nazis responded, and pitched battles raged up and down the beachfront. By the end of the week the Allies controlled a 70-mile strip of coastline. They smashed their way inland to liberate Paris on August 23 and the rest of France by the middle of September. With Russia advancing from

"History records no greater achievement in so limited a time…. The highest honor I have ever attained is that of having my name coupled with yours in these great events."

—*GENERAL GEORGE PATTON,*
to the men of the Third Army, heroes at the Battle of the Bulge
and in the European campaign, March 23, 1945

The landing at Normandy (opposite page) was a decisive moment in the war but many hard-fought battles still lay ahead, from hand-to-hand combat in France (above, left) to the frigid Battle of the Bulge (left) and the exhausting Pacific campaign (above).

the East and Italy falling to the Allies, the beginning of the end for Germany was in sight.

In late 1944 Hitler, against the advice of his generals, launched a desperate counterstrike. He massed 250,000 troops—half the men available to him on the Western Front—and invaded the Ardennes region, targeting the Belgian city of Antwerp. In frigid, snowy conditions, the assault bulged some 50 miles into U.S.-held territory—it became known as the Battle of the Bulge—before reinforcements, led by General George Patton,

News of Germany's defeat brought huge crowds to New York's Times Square (opposite page); but it took the devastation of Hiroshima (above) and Nagasaki to produce the Japanese surrender on board the *U.S.S. Missouri* (right).

arrived and turned the bloody tide. The United States committed 650,000 troops to the battle and suffered a stunning 81,000 casualties.

But the end of the war in Europe was at hand. When Berlin fell in the spring, Hitler committed suicide. The Allies turned their attention to the Pacific, where General Douglas MacArthur and Admiral Chester Nimitz were leading successful, island-hopping offensives. Tokyo was reduced to ashes, but, given an ultimatum to surrender or face invasion, Japan chose to fight on. Rather than risk thousands of American lives in a major assault on Japan, President Harry Truman authorized the use of the atomic bomb, which had been tested in the New Mexico desert in July. The first bomb fell on Hirsohima on August 6, 1945. Three days later a second one devastated Nagasaki. On September 2 on the deck of the *U.S.S. Missouri*, Japan signed an unconditional surrender.

Aftermath

Only a villain as dangerous as Adolf Hitler could have united such strange bedfellows as the United States, the Soviet Union and Britain, and sure enough, when the war was over, the Soviets began to withdraw in pursuit of their own interests. Stalin's forces annexed neighboring lands and ran afoul of the newly established United Nations.

When the Soviets refused to cooperate with the Baruch Plan to regulate nuclear weapons or the Marshall Plan to rebuild war-torn Western Europe, the Cold War began in earnest. The Soviets developed nuclear weapons in 1949 and, with revolution in China, the division of the world into communist East and democratic West was complete and the arms race was under way.

ORIGINAL SLINKY $1.00

SLINKY SOLDIERS $2.00

SLINKY SEAL $1.00

SLINKY HANDCAR $2.00

SLINKY SPIRAL $1.00

SLINKY DOG $2.00

Insist on

Slinky ® Toys

AT YOUR NEAREST TOY COUNTER

JAMES INDUSTRIES, PAOLI, PA.

SLINKY WORM • SLINKY TRAIN • SLINKY JUNIOR • SLINKY EYES • SLINKY BUCKO

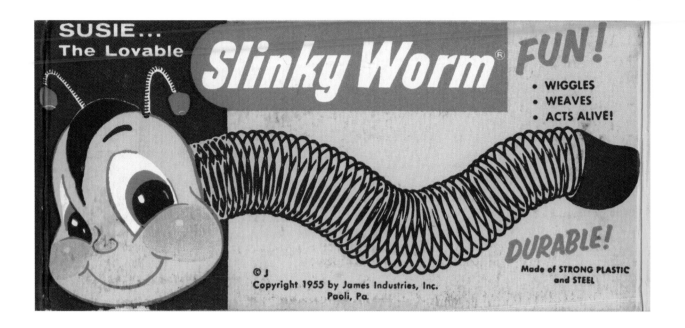

SLINKY

In 1943, while many Americans were at war in Europe and the Pacific, it was just another day at the office for naval engineer Richard James at Philadelphia's Cramp Shipyard. Then a steel torsion spring came loose from a maritime testing meter. The coil bounced harmlessly off a table and the idea sprung forth in James's mind for Slinky, a toy that has charmed children for more than half a century.

That evening James showed the spring to his wife, Betty, and declared, "I think I can make a toy out of this." More than a year of experimentation led to the design formula that allowed the spring to "walk." Seeking a name for the invention, Betty consulted a dictionary and spotted "slink," which, according to the Random House dictionary, means "to move in a slow, provocative, or sinuous way." In 1945 the Jameses

secured a $500 loan to manufacture a small batch of Slinkys to be sold for a dollar each through retail stores in Philadelphia.

Customers initially weren't interested in 80 feet of coiled metal that rested peacefully on the shelf. So to jump-start sales during the Christmas season, the local Gimbel's department store agreed to provide counter space for Richard James to stock 400 Slinkys while he demonstrated his invention. He went down to the store ahead of Betty, who was so afraid that the toy wouldn't sell that she gave a friend a dollar to buy one from her husband.

She could have kept the dollar. Betty entered the toy department and witnessed a mob at the Slinky display waving dollar bills at her husband. All 400 Slinkys were sold within 90 minutes. A later Slinky appearance, at the Macy's flagship store in New

The popular children's toy had many guises, from Slinky Seal and Slinky Dog (left) to Susie the Lovable Slinky Worm (above).

SLINKY® is a registered trademark of James Industries, Inc.

"It's Slinky, it's Slinky, for fun it's a wonderful toy. It's Slinky, it's Slinky, it's fun for a girl and a boy."

—COMMERCIAL JINGLE FOR SLINKY

James Industries promised retailers their share of the Slinky profits (above), whether selling the perennially popular basic model (right) or fancier versions like the Slinky Frog Pull Toy (opposite).

York City, forced the local fire marshal to have the item removed when the clamoring customers created a fire hazard in the overstuffed aisles.

Soon Richard James designed the Slinky manufacturing machines that are still in use today at the company plant in Hollidaysburg, Pennsylvania. In 1946 Slinky was the darling of the American Toy Fair in New York City, and was well on its way to becoming one of the most popular toys ever.

How does Slinky actually walk down stairs, "alone or in pairs"? For a one-piece toy that requires neither batteries nor wind-up, its simple motion is quite complex from a scientific perspective: As the spring proceeds from step to step, energy is transferred along the coil in a compressional or longitudinal wave, similar to a sound wave. Its physical properties, such as length, spring constant, mass of the metal and coil diameter—in addition to the height of the steps—determine how quickly the Slinky moves under the influence of gravity.

But Slinky can do more than just walk down a flight of stairs. According to James Industries, Slinkys have been used as drapery holders, light fixtures, gutter and birdhouse protectors, therapeutic devices, and even a component in pecan-picking machines. During the Korean War, American soldiers tossed Slinkys into trees to function as radio antennas.

For all its uses, Slinky hasn't changed very much over the years. The original blue-black Swedish steel was replaced with a less expensive, silvery American metal, and in 1973 Slinky's ends were crimped for safety reasons. Slinky Jr. was

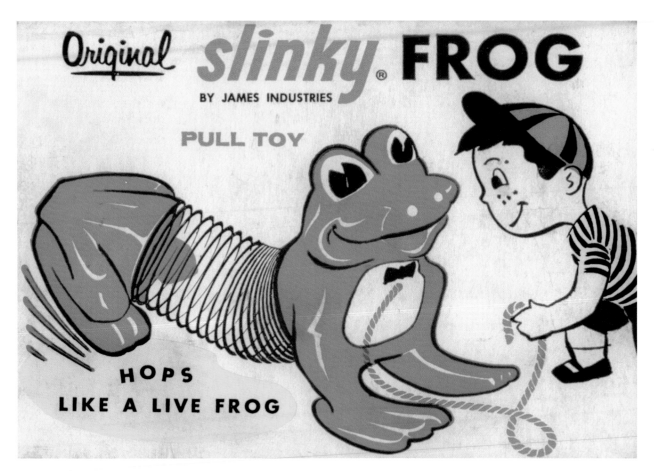

Original Slinky® FROG

BY JAMES INDUSTRIES

PULL TOY

HOPS LIKE A LIVE FROG

introduced in 1950, a dog with a Slinky body in 1955, a plastic model in 1979 and neon-colored plastic Slinkys in 1994. Slinky's cost today? Around two dollars, just twice the 1945 price.

Slinky television commercials debuted on the nascent medium in 1946, and the Slinky jingle ("Everyone Loves a Slinky"), launched in 1962, is one of the most recognizable TV toy jingles in the United States. A 1990 survey found that nearly 90 percent of Americans knew about Slinkys or were familiar with the song. Slinky has even appeared in several films, including *Toy Story* (1995), which featured an updated version of the Slinky Dog.

Since the toy's inception, more than 3,030,000 miles of wire—50,000 tons—have been used to make the classic Slinky and more than 250 million have been sold throughout the world. While most hot toys—from Cabbage Patch Kids to Teenage Mutant Ninja Turtles—are fads that eventually fizzle, Slinky has endured, a testament to its ingenious combination of simplicity, physics and fun.

Aftermath

In a twist worthy of the Slinky coil itself, Mr. James left his wife, six children and James Industries in 1960 to join what Mrs. James described as a religious cult in Bolivia.

The company Betty James inherited was suffering from declining sales and heavy debt. (Richard had sent much of the company's profits to the cult.) Sales rebounded in the late 1970s and '80s when Slinky was introduced to foreign markets. In 1995, to commemorate the toy's 50th anniversary, the company introduced a gold-plated Slinky.

The privately-held company doesn't release sales figures, but one needn't worry about Slinky's future: In a 1996 *New York Times* interview Betty announced that "business was phenomenal."

CITIZEN KANE

Orson Welles's 1941 masterpiece *Citizen Kane* is never far from any discussion of the greatest films of all time. In 1996 the American Film Institute asked 1,500 writers, producers, directors and critics to select the 100 best films in a century of American moviemaking, and they put *Citizen Kane* at the top of their list. Unlike other "100 Greatest" lists that have appeared as the millennium approaches, this one provoked little protest at its selections. Indeed, *Citizen Kane* towers over the history of cinema much as its protagonist, the tycoon Charles Foster Kane, towered over the newspaper industry.

A dazzlingly complex portrait of a powerful but enigmatic figure, *Citizen Kane* unfolds in a series of interlocking flashbacks. These are the divergent and sometimes contradictory memories of five characters who were close to Kane, and they infuse the film with the ambiguity and uncertainty of real life. Innovative techniques like deep focus—which allowed both the foreground and the background of a scene to be in focus—and overlapping dialogue added to this effect, which puts the burden of discerning meaning on the viewer.

Critics praised the cunning structure as well as the acting, the exquisite use of sound and Gregg Toland's groundbreaking cinematography. Welles, the film's 25-year-old producer, director, and co-screenwriter, commands the stormy center of the picture with a virtuoso portrayal of Kane, a newspaper mogul who ages from 28 to 80 during the course of the picture.

Welles's co-writer, Herman Mankiewicz, called *Citizen Kane*'s flashback structure a "prismatic" narrative. We see Kane in many lights, some more flattering than others, but what to make of the whole man? In the '40s, many viewers found the portrait maddeningly inconclusive. Jorge Luis Borges called *Citizen Kane* a labyrinth without a

Welles's swaggering Kane (left) found his foil in Jedediah Leland, the man of decency played by Joseph Cotten (top, left).

Welles and Toland (left, in sunglasses) brought a sepulchral feel to the film's closing scene at Kane's uninhabited mansion, now crowded with the objects of a greedy lifetime; the set was sketched (above) before it was actually built (opposite page).

center. To audiences of the day this was surely not a compliment. Accustomed to films with clearly defined villains and heroes, reliable narrators and an overriding clarity, they wanted a verdict on Charles Foster Kane. Welles apparently wasn't offering one.

And what of the film's central conundrum, the tycoon's dying utterance, "Rosebud"? For the characters in the film, this mystery never unravels, and for the audience, well, the "revelation"

in the film's final frame is the starting point for debate over one of the most dissected, deconstructed and decoded films ever. Is it simply a sentimental O. Henry-style ending, or a symbolic comment on something deeper?

As if these challenges weren't enough to prevent *Citizen Kane* from finding an audience, the picture faced another, more daunting obstacle. Few people disputed that Charles Foster Kane was based on real-life newspaper magnate William Randolph

> "Last Wednesday afternoon I went to see a picture that had the most terrific build-up of any picture ever made. After seeing the picture I felt that everything that had been said was an understatement."
>
> —*SIDNEY SKOLSKY,*
> *film critic, on* Citizen Kane, New York Post, *1941*

Hearst. And Hearst was not pleased with his silver-screen Doppelgänger nor with the portrait Welles painted of Hearst's longtime companion Marion Davies. Wielding a power that seems unimaginable today, Hearst all but suppressed the picture by prohibiting any of his nationwide chain of newspapers, radio stations or wire services from mentioning *Citizen Kane* or any other film released by RKO Radio Pictures. The Hearst influence was so powerful that a group of Hollywood studio heads, afraid of alienating the influential Hearst press, approached RKO with a proposal: one million dollars in exchange for the destruction of the film's negatives and prints.

But Welles had already previewed his movie for too many of the right people for it to be ignored. So RKO released it, albeit in a halting, sputtering fashion. Many theater chains, including 20th Century-Fox, caved in to pressure from Hearst and boycotted the film, preventing a genuine national

Through the course of the film, Welles ages from a youthful entrepreneur (above, middle) to an aged and isolated mogul (opposite page) entombed in his gloomy palace with a birdbrained companion, based allegedly on Hearst's real-life lover Marion Davies. Though Hearst was unhappy with the portrayal of himself, the portait of Davies was said to infuriate him even more.

release and ensuring an utter commercial flop. But critics immediately recognized the landmark status of the film, and Bosley Crowther of *The New York Times* wrote, "Now that the wrappers are off, it can be safely stated that the suppression of this film would have been a crime."

Aftermath

By the time the 1941 Academy Awards ceremony took place, people were apparently tired of the controversy surrounding Welles and his film. Each mention of *Citizen Kane* and its director was booed lustily, and the film, which was nominated for nine Oscars®, won only one, for best screenplay.

The critical response to *Citizen Kane*, however, has remained unchanged in the more than 50 years since its original release. It was hailed as a classic then as now, and its influence on countless directors as diverse as Martin Scorcese, Roger Corman, and Ridley Scott is well documented. The commercial response, too, has been consistent: Rereleased into theaters in 1991 for its 50th anniversary, *Citizen Kane* fared little better than it had the first time around.

THE JITTERBUG

As a veteran on the American music circuit, the great clarinetist Benny Goodman had traveled coast to coast and seen a lot of strange things. Still, nothing prepared him for his first glimpse of the phenomenon known as the jitterbug. "[The dancer's] eyes rolled, his limbs began to spin like a windmill in a hurricane—his attention, riveted to the rhythm, transformed him into a whirling dervish," recalled Goodman, who was sure the dancer was "off his conk."

That was 1934, in Kansas City. But for the next 10 years or so, it could have been anywhere jumping swing music was performed: at the Palomar Ballroom in Los Angeles; the Lakeside Ballroom in Denver; the Palace in Fort Wayne, Indiana; and any number of places in New York City, from Roseland downtown to countless uptown joints like Small's Paradise, Jimmy's Chicken Shack, the Cotton Club and the Savoy Ballroom—especially the Savoy, for that was where many of the wildest

dance steps originated. The Savoy had its own traveling dance team, Whitey's Lindy Hoppers, who were hired out to other ballrooms under the billing "Whitey's Hopping Maniacs" and who also performed frequently at lavish downtown parties.

Dancers all over the country worked feverishly to imitate Whitey's team, executing the acrobatic dance known as either the jitterbug, the Lindy or the Lindy Hop, the last two in honor of Charles Lindbergh's historic flight across the Atlantic. More than any dance before it, the jitterbug placed a premium on athletic inventiveness, and it was perfectly normal for dancers to finish the evening bathed in sweat. "You don't see a whole ballroom moving sedately around in the same direction with the same steps—ice skating style," said music critic Mike Levin. "You see some very good and very bad stabs at really original styles."

Crowds, musicians and dancers worked together,

Kids (opposite page) strove to imitate the flashy moves of early pioneers such as Whitey's Lindy Hoppers (above).

The jitterbug was performed in every conceivable venue, from the beach in Venice, California (right), to a Jimmy Dorsey concert at New York's Roxy Theater (opposite page, right), to a jitterbug contest at the 1939 New York World's Fair (opposite page, left), to a tiny juke joint outside Clarksdale, Mississippi (above).

"The first swing-out was like madness. It was every man for himself. The loud yell from the dancers meant it was on. They made noises similar to those of martial arts, the sound that releases pent-up energy."

—*NORMA MILLER, early Lindy Hopper*

inciting each other to new feats of flash and daring. Young Malcolm X, an enthusiastic Lindy Hopper during his wild early days in Boston, described the frenzy that often seized dancers: "A band was screaming when she kicked off her shoes and got barefooted, and shouted, and shook herself as if she were in some African jungle frenzy, and then she let loose with some dancing, shouting with every step until the guy that was out there with her had to fight her to control her. The crowd loved any way-out lindying style that made a colorful show like that."

Of course, not everyone was happy about all this, especially those who thought middle-class white kids were experiencing "African jungle frenzy." Many critics saw an alarming parallel between the swing-induced delirium on dance floors across the United States and fascist brainwashing overseas. One social scientist at Barnard College called the music's strange power over its initiates "musical Hitlerism," and Francis J. L. Beckman, the Catholic archbishop of Dubuque, Iowa, denounced swing as an evil force in young people's lives. "We permit jam sessions, jitterbug and cannibalistic rhythmic orgies

Eye-catching moves like the one at left graced dance halls such as Roseland (above, right), the Orpheum (above, left) and the Mardi Gras swing casino at the World's Fair in New York (opposite page, left); the dance floor was one place where a segregated society saw its racial barriers crossed (opposite page, right).

to occupy a place in our social scheme of things, wooing our youth along the primrose path to hell."

The kids loved it. For the first time, they had their own culture, with its own distinctive music, lingo, dance steps and fashion. For girls, the jitterbug uniform consisted of saddle shoes, bobbysocks and skirts full enough to permit the wilder maneuvers. Boys often wore "zoot suits"—single breasted jackets with narrow waists and broad shoulders, trousers with narrow cuffs and superwide knees, producing a "pegged" effect. The look was decidedly lower class, even criminal, and it scandalized the public.

Dance crazes come and go, of course, but as dancer George Wendler has pointed out, since the jitterbug, there hasn't been much interest in conservative popular dances. There was a racial undertone to the whole phenomenon, of course, with dancers of all hues jumping deftly back and forth across the color line to choose favorite bands and dance partners. In fact, the name jitterbug comes from blacks' describing the awkward movements white people made while doing black dances.

At first called just "the Hop," the dance seems to

have been some newfangled variation on the Charleston. To do the jitterbug, dancers held each other relatively far apart and used the freedom and roominess of swing's 4/4 tempo to execute "the breakaway," the style's most eye-catching maneuver which could be a backflip, a snatch, or an over-the-head leap as the man tossed his trusting partner skyward. Credit for developing the jitterbug goes mostly to a Harlem dancer named Shorty Snowdon, but the breakaway was probably the brainstorm of his protégé, Frankie Manning, who made dance history by executing the first one during a friendly competition with Snowdon.

"So I swung Frieda out, man, and I jump over her head, you know. When I jumped over her head [band leader], Chick Webb say, boom. And then when I turn and she hit my back and I flipped over and she hit the floor right on the music, and as she hit the floor Chick Webb say, 'Damn!' I say, 'Yeah man, we got them now.'"

Aftermath

Dance moves are rarely invented from whole cloth. Instead they are recycled and revamped from generation to generation under new names. While the jitterbug and other swing dances began to lose popularity in the late 1940s, they were resurrected about 15 years later on the many popular television dance shows for teens, such as *American Bandstand* **and** *Hullabaloo.* **Elements of the Charleston were visible in the Mashed Potato, and the Chicken appeared to borrow some of its moves from the Lindy. Of course, it can be blinding to stare across the generation gap, and those old Lindy Hoppers were scandalized to see what their kids were up to.**

ABSTRACT EXPRESSIONISM

Today Abstract Expressionism is widely acknowledged as America's first visual arts movement of international significance. Yet very few people knew what to make of this school of art when it exploded out of New York City during the decade of the '40s. The images on canvas were startling. Indeed, most were more primal shapes than recognizable images—bold, raw and seemingly unfinished. They jumped off the canvas in an explosion of color and energy, ignited, it seemed, by the same brash spirit of adventure that had settled the American wilderness. You couldn't ignore the new painting, but you didn't have to like it. In 1959 the critic John Canaday sniffed that the school's popularity was based on "the premise that wild unintelligibility alone places a contemporary artist in line with great men who were misunderstood by their contemporaries."

The United States had emerged from World War II as the world's foremost power. Its economic and military might were unrivaled, and its culture—films, jazz, and architecture—was rapidly redefining aesthetics around the world. Abstract Expressionism was the first flexing of American might in the visual arts. As art critic Clement Greenberg proclaimed in 1948, "The main premises of Western art have at last migrated to the United States." For some years already, established European artists like Marc Chagall, Piet Mondrian and Yves Tanguy had been fleeing the Old World for the New. Suddenly, New York displaced Paris as the acknowledged capital of the art world.

Out of this ferment came Abstract Expressionism. Among the artists now classified as Abstract Expressionists are Jackson Pollock, Barnett Newman, Robert Motherwell, Mark Rothko, Willem de Kooning and Lee Krasner. As art critic Robert

Pollock (above) and Rothko, who created the evocative *Untitled, 1949* (left), were two of the school's masters.

"Sometimes, as in his [Pollock's] masterpiece, *Number 1, 1948,* the whirling vortex of lines develops a mysterious glow of light, without however destroying the sense of picture surface which Pollock and all his companions seek to preserve as essential to art."

—*ALFRED H. BARR, JR., art critic, 1950*

Though Krasner's work (*Noon,* 1947, opposite page) never received attention equal to her husband's, she is widely credited with enabling the heavy-drinking Pollock to keep producing brilliant paintings like *Number 1A, 1948* (above).

Hughes pointed out, the label Abstract Expressionism was really more a critic's convenience than anything else, since there was little formal similarity between the rich, blurry colors in Rothko's *Untitled* (1949) and the frenetic lines of de Kooning's *Excavation* (1950), and between the swirls and

spatters of Pollock's "drip" paintings and Barnett Newman's "zip" paintings, with their trademark vertical lines cutting through a solid field. Still, those painters and their lesser known contemporaries spent a lot of time in each other's company, arguing art world politics and theory and drinking at Greenwich Village hangouts like the Cedar Tavern and the Waldorf Cafeteria. Many had their first big shows at Peggy Guggenheim's Art of This Century gallery.

Though the New York School shocked people, it had clear roots in Europe's more established school of Paris abstraction and Surrealism. In fact, to a significant degree Abstract Expressionists saw themselves as miners of the unconscious. Explained the painter Adolph Gottlieb, "One had to dig into one's self, excavate whatever one could, and if what came out did not seem to be art by accepted standards, so much the worse for the accepted standards."

While Abstract Expressionism owed a great deal to Surrealism, it went further in the exploration of gestural abstraction and non-objective painting. As strange and disturbing as Surrealism could be, there was no mistaking even its wildest images: Those melting ovals Salvador Dali painted were watches and nothing else. Abstract Expressionism, wrote David and Cecile Shapiro in their introduction to *Abstract Expressionism:*

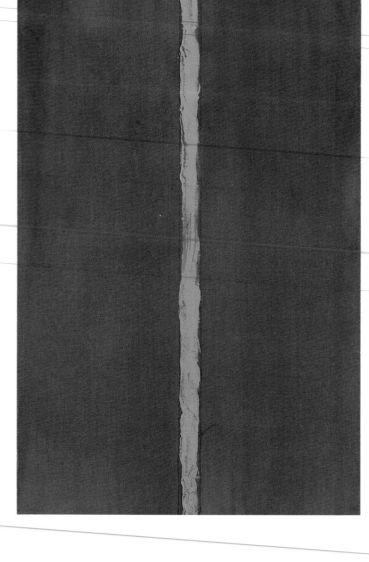

Rothko's earlier work such as *Baptismal Scene*, 1945 (above), showed a debt to Surrealism, while the paintings of de Kooning (*Excavation*, 1950, opposite page) and Newman (*Onement*, 1948, right) demonstrated the broad spectrum of styles encompassed by Abstract Expressionism.

A Critical Record, "dispensed with recognizable images from the known world. Its surfaces were often rough, unfinished, even sloppy, with uneven textures and dripping paint."

During the decade of the 1940s, Jackson Pollock became the undisputed leader of the Abstract Expressionist movement. Born in Cody, Wyoming in 1912, Pollock moved to New York in 1930 to study with the American Regionalist painter Thomas Hart Benton. By the late '40s Pollock had forged his mature style in which he dripped and poured paint onto canvases laid flat on the floor of his studio in East Hampton, Long Island.

"On the floor I am more at ease," he explained. "I feel nearer, more a part of the painting, since this way I can walk around it, work from the four sides and literally be *in* the painting. This is akin to the method of the Indian sand painters of the West." Sarcastically dubbed "Jack the Dripper" by *Time,* Pollock was in constant motion while at work, walking around the canvas, dripping, flinging and pouring paint on it with an unusual array of tools. "I prefer sticks, trowels, knives and dripping fluid paint or a heavy impasto with

sand, broken glass or other foreign matter added."

Pollock was a heavy drinker, and many historians credit his wife and fellow Abstract Expressionist painter Lee Krasner with keeping his career on track for the better part of their life together. Pollock died in 1956, at the age of 44, when the car he was drunkenly driving sped off the road. All too soon it was possible to follow the sardonic advice Pollock gave those who claimed not to understand him: to visit his grave and "try just listening. You can feel what I'm trying to say, maybe." The art world is still listening, attentively.

Aftermath

Today Jackson Pollock is considered one of the most influential and innovative painters of the twentieth century. In 1994, the artist's home and studio was designated a National Historic Landmark. Owned and operated by the State University of New York at Stony Brook, the Pollock-Krasner House and Study Center is open to the public by appointment. In 1998 *New York* magazine dubbed the paint laden floor of Pollock's East Hampton studio "the most famous floor in America."

WOMEN SUPPORT WAR EFFORT

While American women have always worked outside the home, the importance of female workers to the nation's security and prosperity was celebrated as never before during World War II. The military had drained the work force of men and the government was calling for the intense production of war matériel. In 1942 the recently created War Manpower Commission recognized that the labor shortage could be alleviated only with the commitment of "womanpower" to the war effort.

More than six million women joined the work force during the war, while countless numbers of the 12 million women already in the work force left low-status and low-paying jobs to take advantage of the unprecedented opportunities in the defense industries.

Women, reported *Newsweek* in August 1943, "are in the shipyards, lumber mills, steel mills, foundries. They are welders, electricians, mechanics, and even boilermakers. They operate street-

cars, buses, cranes, and tractors. Women engineers are working in the drafting rooms and women physicists and chemists in the great industrial laboratories." While hardly inclusive of the full range of jobs women took on, this list indicates the inroads they made into fields popularly assumed to require "masculine" capabilities. "Rosie the Riveter," the character who first appeared in a song written by Redd Evans and John Jacob Loeb in 1942, became the standard-bearer for women employed in the defense industries, and stories and images published in magazines, newspapers, and recruitment posters portrayed women in overalls, workshirts and with muscles—as well as lipstick and mascara.

Indeed, part of the strategy of the Office of War Information, which worked with the War Manpower Commission to overcome prejudices against women in the workplace, was to stress women's ability to maintain their femininity as

Women, who took to factory work like never before (above and left), helped to ensure an Allied victory.

they mastered the technology that made the United States what President Roosevelt called "the great arsenal for democracy." The film *Glamour Girls of '43*, for example, described factory work in unthreatening domestic terms: "Instead of cutting the lines of a dress, this woman cuts the pattern of aircraft parts. Instead of baking cake, this woman is cooking gears to reduce the tension in the gears after use.... After a short apprenticeship, this woman can operate a drill press just as easily as a juice extractor in her own kitchen."

However it was phrased, the call for female workers was music to the ears of the hundreds of thousands of women who had been hit especially hard during the Depression, when the job shortage had made employers even less willing than usual to hire them. Not only did job opportunities for women suddenly proliferate, but the jobs created by the war were also compensated as traditionally female occupations never were.

The Women's Bureau of the Department of Labor found that in Detroit, for example, women who worked in defense industries took home an average $40.35 a week while women who worked in laundries and restaurants or as clerks took home from $24.10 to $29.75 a week. African-American women in particular seized the chance to escape from dead-end jobs as domestic servants. "The war made me live better, it really did. My sister always said that Hitler was the one that got us out of the white folks' kitchen," said Fanny Christina Hill, whose career at North American Aircraft in Los Angeles began during the war and lasted until her retirement in 1980.

While those who worked in the defense indus-

tries received most of the attention, women contributed to the war effort in virtually every arena. Some took "essential civilian" jobs—as taxi and bus drivers, bank tellers, police officers—to keep everyday life running smoothly. Three hundred fifty thousand women joined newly created branches of the military. While most of them served as clerical workers and nurses, one thousand women flew commercial and air force transport planes; and toward the end of the war many

70

"Going to work during the war changed me—made me grow up a little and realize I could do things. Look what I've done since. It's quite a change."

—*MARIE BAKER, a worker at North American Aircraft*

Answering government calls for increased weapons production (inset), women such as the welders above assumed jobs formerly reserved for men but lost none of their glamour (opposite page).

In support of the war effort food ration stamps were issued (above), victory garden produce was canned (far left), cooking fats were used to make explosives (left) and extra pots and pans were collected to be melted down (opposite page).

others joined the men overseas. On the home front millions volunteered for the Red Cross and Civilian Defense. Homemakers contended with the rationing of such essentials as butter, sugar and shoes. They salvaged scrap metal, newspapers, cooking fats, rubber, aluminum, tin cans, and nylon and silk stockings to be reused in making everything from bombs to gunpowder to parachutes. They planted "victory gardens" that produced up to one-third of all vegetables grown in the country. Because the war effort had so pervaded every aspect of life, including what homemakers put on the table for dinner, when victory finally came, women knew they had helped to achieve it.

Aftermath

Although surveys in 1944 showed that 75 to 80 percent of women working in defense industries planned to continue working and hoped to keep their jobs after the war, by 1946 three million women of an estimated 19 million in such jobs had left the work force, some to go home voluntarily, others because they had been laid off in favor of returning servicemen. The women who stayed in the work force were encouraged—and often forced—to return to traditionally female-dominated and lower-paying occupations. In the end, the net increase of women participating in the work force after the war was consistent with previous trends. Nonetheless, the strength and skill displayed by women in the war effort served as an inspiration for a generation of feminists who succeeded them.

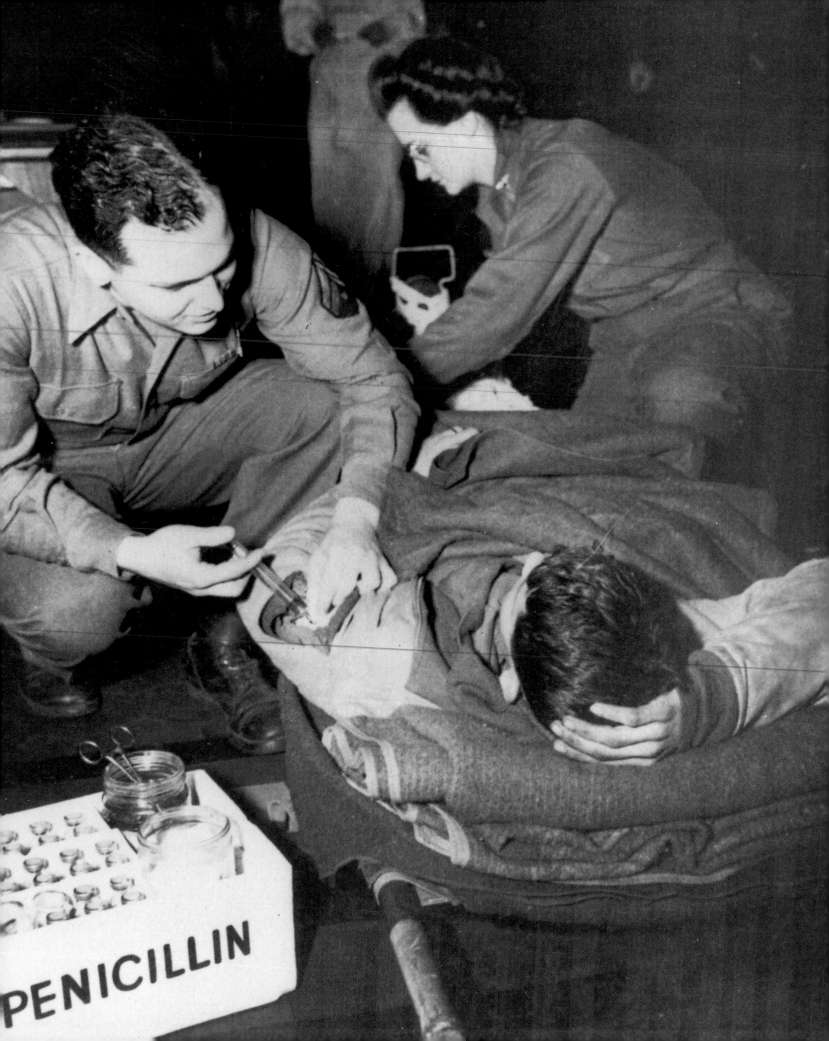

PENICILLIN

ANTIBIOTICS SAVE LIVES

During World War I, 15 percent of all deaths were the result of infected wounds. In World War II by contrast, from D-Day until the collapse of Germany, the death rate from infection among Allied soldiers was near zero. The difference: penicillin. So effective was this first antibiotic that many cite it as a major factor in defeating the Germans, who relied on far less effective sulfa drugs for treating battle diseases like gangrene, pneumonia and septicemia.

That penicillin was readily available by D-Day was something of a miracle. In fact, if not for an errant mold spore that lighted on a petri dish belonging to Scottish bacteriologist Alexander Fleming at St. Mary's Hospital in London in September 1928, it is possible, if hard to conceive, that we might still today be without benefit of this miracle drug. As with much of

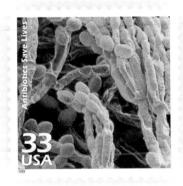

medical history, there are many versions of the story surrounding the discovery of penicillin. It is certain, though, that Fleming observed a mold contaminant killing the pathogens he had cultured in a petri dish. He reasoned that this mold, which he identified as penicillin, must contain or produce something that would kill the same organisms in a human host, provided it was not toxic to the host.

The implications for medical science were immense. But lacking chemical expertise and unable to rally sufficient support or interest, Fleming could not purify the highly unstable microorganism for clinical use. The tremendous promise of penicillin remained untapped for 12 years until a team of Oxford scientists led by Howard Florey and Ernst Chain successfully achieved purification. On May 25, 1940, they began testing the drug on infected

Penicillin, the miracle drug discovered by Fleming (above), saved countless lives (left) during World War II.

"The discovery of penicillin...revolutionized medicine and largely removed the scourge of once killer diseases...."

—MILTON WAINWRIGHT,
author of Miracle Cure: The Story of Antibiotics, *1990*

Florey (right) and Chain (bottom) purified penicillin (right, below) and first tested it on humans; streptomycin, prepared in a sterile environment by lab technicians at Merck (opposite page) and discovered by Waksman (top) and Schatz, provided the first cure for once deadly tuberculosis.

mice. Early the following year they demonstrated the effectiveness of penicillin on human patients, albeit on a limited scale. But the process of extracting the fragile active ingredient was painstaking and slow, and the mass production necessary for large-scale testing seemed eons away, especially given Great Britain's preoccupation with the war.

Florey found the support he needed at the Northern Regional Research Laboratory (NRRL) in Peoria, Illinois, where an ideal medium (corn steep liquor) and a better producing strain of the mold (the so-called "cantaloupe strain" that came from a local fruit market) were quickly found. In 1943 the U.S. War Production Board made the mass production of penicillin its highest development priority after the atomic bomb. U.S. laboratories and manufacturers worked furiously in a coordinated effort with British counterparts. Using a deep fermentation process developed by the NRRL, the United States was able to produce 21 billion units of lifesaving penicillin in 1943. By 1944, Allied supplies of the antibiotic were described as "unlimited." Just three years earlier, supplies had been so scarce that penicillin was extracted from patients' urine for reuse. Indeed, penicillin likely would have remained a laboratory curiosity for many years had it not been for the exigencies of war.

But if the troops were well supplied with the

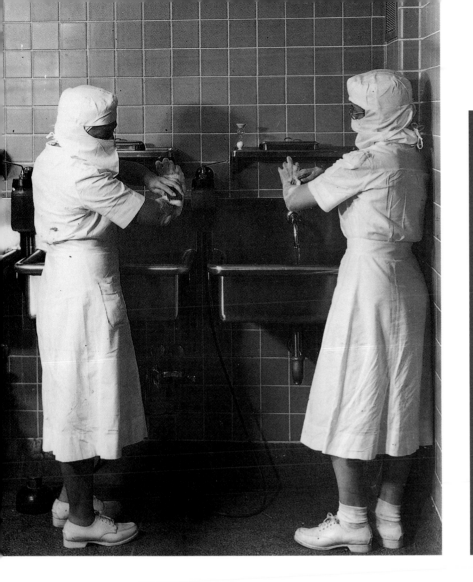

Aftermath

The average American born today can expect to live 21 years longer than those born in 1920. Roughly 10 of those years can be attributed to antibiotics. But overuse of these pathogen-fighting drugs has led to a serious problem of bacterial resistance. Broad concern that our arsenal of weapons to combat drug-resistant bacteria is rapidly shrinking has caused large companies to return to antibiotic research. The World Health Organization has predicted that vaccines will someday replace antibiotics. Another promising area of study is "bacteriotherapy," or probiotics, in which nonpathogenic bacteria outcompete pathogens. In the meantime, prevention through increased public health measures, especially in developing countries, appears more critical than ever.

wonder drug, civilians were not, as reflected in 1943 headlines like "U.S. Delays Penicillin's Civilian Use," and "Penicillin Helps Boy; Is Denied Woman." Priority was given to acute cases of bacterial infection. To meet public demand, the manufacture of crude penicillin resumed.

A seeming miracle in an age when people could die of something as benign as a finger prick from a rose thorn, penicillin nonetheless fell short of being a medical panacea. Resistant strains of bacteria developed; cases of fatal allergies to the drug were reported; and for all the illnesses penicillin cured, such as meningitis, puerperal fever and pneumonia, it was impotent against the leading cause of death in the United States: tuberculosis. Fortunately, penicillin had opened the doors wide for the discovery of other antibiotics. By 1944 the

first tuberculosis cure commenced with streptomycin, a new antibiotic that was discovered by soil microbiologist Selman Abraham Waksman and his research assistant Albert Schatz. The golden age of antibiotics had begun. Pharmaceutical companies, motivated as much by money as by humanitarian concerns, began extensive screening programs that yielded chloramphenicol (1947) and chlortetracycline (1948), for example.

Penicillin has since undergone myriad refinements and remains the world's most widely used antibiotic. While perhaps not perfect, antibiotics, which saved some 80,000 lives in their first 10 years of widespread availability, are a vast improvement over the more bizarre forms of antibacterial treatment, like live maggot therapy, that preceded them.

THE BIG BAND SOUND

As even the dullest of cats must know by now, "it don't mean a thing if it ain't got that swing." But what exactly is swing? Is it a feeling or is it a thing? The great clarinetist and band leader Benny Goodman defined swing as "collective improvisation, rhythmically integrated." But one of his fans may have done him one better when she defined it as "syncopated raw emotion."

"To know what swing is," Goodman said, "you have to feel it inside." In other words, if you have to ask, you'll never know. Swing was the ultimate insider's club, with its own heroes, dance steps and fashions, its own specialist magazines like *Downbeat* and radio shows like "Make Believe Ballroom"—even its own ultrahip language.

Coming between the bluesy New Orleans jazz of Louis Armstrong and the wild experimentations of bebop innovators like Charlie Parker, swing was orchestral jazz, jumping with syncopated rhythms and glorying in improvisation. It was the sound of a nation throwing off the misery and shrunken hopes of the Depression and joyously cutting loose. Some, apparently threatened by its roots in African-American music, dismissed it as primitive "jungle" music. Listen to Gene Krupa's drum solo that opens Goodman's radical reworking of Louis Prima's "Sing, Sing, Sing," and you'll know they were at least partially right. Swing was indeed wild music, hellbent on going as far as it could in the pursuit of a jumping groove.

Musically, swing's loose 4/4 tempo left more room for improvisation and fancy dance steps than had the 2/4 tempo of earlier popular music. Another distinguishing feature of swing was its call-and-response arrangements, borrowed from black work songs and gospel, in which whole sections, acting as a single voice, would echo and respond to one another.

The call-and-response structure is prominent in

Duke Ellington (opposite page) and Glenn Miller (above) were two of the most popular practitioners of swing.

two of the most famous of all swing arrangements, Duke Ellington's "Take the 'A' Train" and Glenn Miller's "In the Mood," in which the reeds play a mellow line only to be answered by the more insistent, aggressive horns.

Swing offered young people of all races and classes a common language, as high-school and college students across America rejected their parents' culture in favor of building their own. During the Depression the most popular entertainers had been crooners like Rudy Vallee and Bing Crosby and their female equivalent, the torch singer, all of whom specialized in a style

one wag wittily dismissed as the "first popularization of that well-known modern vice, the inferiority complex." The music began to sound tired and defeated, much like the times. The other popular performers were the so-called "sweet" bands like Guy Lombardo and his Royal Canadians, whose musical aim was also to soothe rather than to excite. Even trumpet player Max Kaminsky claimed that whenever he tried to alleviate the boredom of playing with the NBC orchestra by injecting a little "hot" jazz, its conductor, Leo Reisman, would shake his finger in furious warning and hiss, "You're *playing!*"

> "Swing is the voice of youth striving to be heard in this fast-moving world of ours. Swing is the tempo of our time. Swing is real. Swing is alive."
>
> —THE NEW YORK TIMES, *1939*

Swing gloried in such playing. Whenever a band would launch into a "killer-diller," fans would urge the players on with ecstatic shouts. Battles of the bands were popular competitive events, musical heavyweight bouts. When Goodman took his band uptown to Harlem's Savoy Ballroom—the "Home of Happy Feet"—to do battle with the Chick Webb Orchestra, the place would be packed to the rafters. Though swing music had many successful white band leaders and players, like Goodman, Miller, Artie Shaw and the Dorsey brothers, there is no doubt that swing was based on black American music. Goodman, whose background as a poor Jewish kid from Chicago seems to have given him special insight into prejudice, was the first band leader to integrate his band. "We were the first interracial organization in this country," claimed Goodman's black piano player, Teddy Wilson, noting that jazz fans "were just hungry for this sort of thing."

Ellington had a special appeal for both black and white fans. "Ellington was the epitome of black urban sophistication," said one fan. "He was what men dreamed of becoming and women dreamed of possessing." Born in Washington,

Swing went overseas with the troops via recordings from bands such as Count Basie's (above), concerts by swing stars like Shaw (opposite page) and special broadcasts by celebrities such as Dinah Shore, Spike Jones, Basie, Bob Burns, Lionel Hampton and Tommy Dorsey (top, left to right).

D.C., to a middle-class family, the Duke had lofty aims for his music. He hoped, in the words of swing historian Lewis A. Erenberg, "to blend the African past and the European classical tradition to enrich African-American culture." To this day, many would say he succeeded brilliantly.

But the most commercially successful of all swing band leaders was Miller, who took Goodman's crown in 1939 and held it fast for the next five years. Born in Iowa and raised in Colorado, Miller was able to take the new urban music and sell it to middle America. By consciously striving for a commercial blend of pretty music and jumping swing, Miller had a slew of hits beyond "In the Mood," including "Tuxedo Junction," "String of Pearls" and "Chattanooga Choo-Choo," which in 1942 became the first record to sell a million copies.

An unabashed patriot, Miller became a hero when he gave up his extremely lucrative career to join the army in September 1942. Recognizing that the greatest weapon Miller could wield was

Crowds flocked to listen to the intoxicating sounds of swing from the likes of Jimmy Dorsey (below, left), Krupa (below) and Webb (left); Goodman (opposite page), the first white star to integrate his band, drew fans both black and white to hear his wailing clarinet solos.

probably his baton, the army had him put together a series of bands, the most famous of which, the Army Air Force Orchestra, toured nonstop, bringing quintessentially American music to soldiers far from home. "America means freedom and there's no expression of freedom quite so sincere as music," said Miller. When his small plane went down over the English Channel on December 15, 1944, the country mourned one of its most beloved heroes, the man who had made swing the all-American music.

Aftermath

Inspired in part by the 1997 movie *Swingers,* swing music has enjoyed a recent renaissance, with bands like the Royal Crown Revue, the Cherry Poppin' Daddies, Big Voodoo Daddy and the Squirrel Nut Zippers working their own variations on the original style. Clubs like the Derby in Los Angeles, built by Cecil B. De Mille in 1929, feature nouveau swing, which, for the most part, is harder edged than the "real" thing, borrowing almost as much from rockabilly as from Benny Goodman.

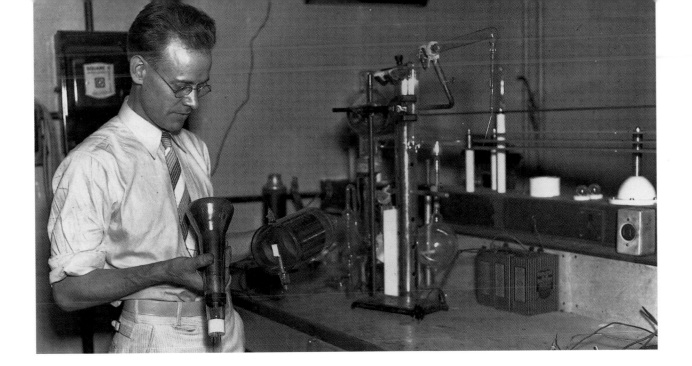

TV ENTERTAINS AMERICA

Certainly most Americans can name the inventor of the light bulb, but how many can say who created the first television? Glowing for six hours a day in the average U.S. household, TV has had at least as transforming an effect on the culture as Edison's breakthrough, yet its inventor is virtually unknown. Indeed, in 1957, the father of television, Philo T. Farnsworth, appeared on the TV program *I've Got a Secret* and won $50 for stumping the contestants. No one knew who he was or what he had done.

The inventor's anonymity is in keeping with the early history of television, a medium that was vastly underestimated at the start. Farnsworth, who like Edison was a prodigy, laid the groundwork for TV when he was only 16 years old and went on to invent a baby incubator and the fax machine. Yet, as he and his television made their way in the world, neither was accorded due respect.

Farnsworth was bullied by corporate giant RCA, which challenged his patent claims for television; and TV was disdained by most of the people who came in contact with it—including those who appeared on the early tube. Newsman Hugh Downs admitted he thought TV was "just a gimmick" when he started in the industry in Chicago in 1943. Orrin Dunlap, the radio editor for *The New York Times*, dismissed television as "an inventor's will-o'-the-wisp."

Even the cognoscenti were blind to television's possibilities. When Moss Hart, president of the New York Dramatists Guild, called a meeting in the mid-'40s to discuss what he saw in the emerging medium of television, the guild members all

Although initially maligned, the new invention by Philo Farnsworth (above) was an instant winner among children (left).

but laughed in his face. Hart insisted there could one day be a demand for writers to crank out teleplays by the dozen each week. When he finished speaking, an older member of the guild raised his hand. "Where was it ever decreed that man had to have so much entertainment?" the writer asked.

If only Farnsworth's contemporaries of the 1920s had understood the prophetic nature of one of the first images he transmitted through his invention: a dollar sign. By the 1940s advertisers had recognized TV's potential for reaching consumers, and the giants of radio broadcasting began to channel their energies to the new medium. TV took off. Roughly 8,000 American homes had television sets in 1945. Three years later Milton Berle attracted an audience of nearly five million for his Tuesday night

> ## "Milton really started the business. Tuesday night, theaters and restaurants were empty. Everybody was home watching Berle."
>
> —AARON RUBEN, *TV writer*

Sid Caesar and Imogene Coca's classic comedy program *Your Show of Shows* (right, above) set new standards of excellence; comic Milton Berle (far right) and wrestler Gorgeous George (near right) attracted millions of viewers; *Howdy Doody* (opposite) was so popular with children that it quickly went from a weekly to a daily program.

vaudeville show, *Texaco Star Theater*.

Berle's biggest ratings rival, former gossip columnist Ed Sullivan, debuted with his variety show in '48 and stayed on the air until 1971. In 1949 Sid Caesar's radio show jumped to television under the name *Admiral Broadway Revue*. (Admiral was a TV set manufacturer.) The following year NBC picked up the show and, instead of seeking a corporate sponsor, sold advertising by the minute, as a magazine sells ad space. This changed the industry. Now titled *Your Show of Shows*, the program further revolutionized the new medium by the standard of excellence it set. The cast included Caesar, Imogene Coca, Carl Reiner, writer Mel Brooks, as well as top musical talent from Broadway.

While these productions ushered in the Golden Age of television, two other types of programming provided the industry's bread and butter: children's shows and sports. Former radio personality Bob Smith took to the airwaves on Saturday afternoons on NBC with a red-haired, freckle-faced puppet whose signature greeting, "Howdy doody, boys and girls!" drew the

nation's youth to the TV set with hypnotic force. Soon the show aired six days a week, and within a decade, sales of Howdy Doody merchandise exceeded $24 million. Baseball games and boxing matches were both popular attractions, but, curiously enough, the "sport" that did as much for TV as Berle had was wrestling. Leading the way was the ludicrous figure of Gorgeous George, a hulking platinum blond in a silk cape.

Alas, programming was almost beside the point in the early days of television. As a young girl of the era recalled, "We were the first ones in the area to have it. Everybody came to look at it. Even if all they saw was a test pattern with no sound, they would sit there and watch."

Aftermath

The idea of a TV station concluding its broadcast day by playing the national anthem seems impossibly quaint nowadays—not the playing of the national anthem, but the closing of the programming day. Imagine! Turning on the TV and being bombarded by nothing more than a cruciform test pattern.

Ninety-eight percent of American homes have at least one television, and TV's evolution is far from complete. The current analog system will soon be replaced by digital technology, and televisions and computers may soon merge, thereby creating a single unit combining television and the internet. Of course, no matter how sophisticated TV becomes, some things will never change: Pro wrestling is still a staple of the industry—complete with a '90s version of Gorgeous George, named Ravishing Rick Rude.

NBC staff prepare titles and visual effects for an experimental show (opposite, below); once TV took off, viewers could watch **everything from election returns (above) to baseball games (top, right) and beauty contests (opposite, above).**

THE GI BILL

Of all the landmark legislation passed during the four administrations of President Franklin D. Roosevelt, one of the most profound and far-reaching was Public Law 346, known more formally as the Servicemen's Readjustment Act of 1944 and more pithily as the GI Bill. Even at a cost of $5.5 billion, the GI Bill has paid for itself over and over again, proving that when a government invests wisely and generously in its people, it can utterly transform the quality of their lives.

Signed into law by President Roosevelt on June 22, 1944, the GI Bill made a number of promises to the 16 million soldiers who had served in World War II. At the time, its main feature seemed to be a program enrolling veterans in the "52-20 Club"—a guarantee of $20 a week for a year upon their return home. But from our vantage point today, it is clear that the GI Bill had two far more lasting provisions. First, by guaranteeing loans for homes and businesses, it converted the United States from a nation of renters to one of homeowners, greatly expanding the middle class and moving the populace from the city to the suburbs. By 1950 more than two million loans had been made. Even more significant, by paying for up to four years of college education to qualified veterans, it raised the sights of all Americans, giving real meaning to the old American promise of equal opportunity.

"College," said Les Faulk, a veteran from Turtle Creek, Pennsylvania, "that was for the teachers' kids or preachers' kids. For the rest of us, with names like Tarantini and Trkula, it was a distant dream."

Much of the credit for the bill's passage goes to the American Legion, which lobbied for it relentlessly. But veterans were also fortunate to have a friend in the White House. As an assistant secretary to the navy during World War I, Roosevelt knew well the challenges that faced returning veterans, and in a 1943 fireside chat he made it clear that they

Returning GIs, like those at Wayne State (left) and Indiana (above), gladly endured close quarters to get a college degree.

wouldn't be forgotten: "Veterans must not be demobilized into an environment of inflation and unemployment, to a place on a bread line or on a corner selling apples. We must this time have plans ready."

But it was not generosity alone that produced the GI Bill. The consequences of not being ready had been made painfully clear 11 years earlier, when in the throes of the Depression the 20,000 World War I vets known as the Bonus Army descended on Washington, D.C., in hopes of persuading Congress to accelerate the bonus payment of $500 they were due to receive in 1944. A pitched battle between veterans and the police persuaded President Hoover to call out the army, and the nation had to endure the sickening spectacle of tanks aimed at U.S. citizens in the streets of the capital. Despite the specter of similar unrest, there were those who argued that the bill's guarantees would produce indolence. In the end the bill passed by a single vote, after a heroic all-night race by Congressman John Gibson from his home in Georgia back to Washington, D.C., to cast that vote.

The veterans who benefited from the GI Bill did not just get through college, they flourished there, in many cases despite the obvious hardship of having to juggle academics with the responsibilities of raising a family. At Stanford, where homecoming veterans swelled the student body from 3,000 to 7,000 and forced the university to convert a former military hospital into a dormitory, veteran scholars were resentfully known as "DARs—Damn Average Raisers." Having survived a war and been given a chance they never thought they'd get, the new students were diligent and ambitious. Of the many veterans of World War II assisted by the bill, 450,000 became engineers, 240,000 accountants, 238,000 teachers, 91,000 scientists and 67,000 doctors. By 1960 roughly half the members of Congress had been educated on the GI Bill. Returning women and African-Americans, who had not previously

"What the GI Bill did was it gave us the qualifications or the credentials to compete for jobs that would ultimately lead us into the middle class. Once we had access to education, to knowledge, to skill, we could upgrade ourselves."

—HARRY BELAFONTE, singer and veteran

The huge influx of servicemen—many of them married, with children—forced colleges to resort to novel housing solutions, such as the somewhat cramped trailers (above and left) at Indiana University and the Quonset huts employed by Northwestern (opposite page).

attended college in great numbers, made their first great impact on campuses, with 60,000 and 70,000, respectively, going to college.

In 1994, on the 50th anniversary of the GI Bill, journalist Edward Kiester Jr., whose own college education had been paid for by the bill, returned to tiny Turtle Creek, Pennsylvania, for his 50th high-school reunion and saw all around him evidence of the bill's success. Of his 103 male classmates, 30 had earned college degrees, almost 10 times the school's previous high. Twenty-eight had earned their degrees through the GI Bill, among them 10 engineers, two physicists, three professors, an entomologist and a microbiologist.

The top two students in the Turtle Creek class of 1945 were Bill Norris and Layman Allen. Though exceedingly bright, the two good friends had aspired

to nothing more than managerial jobs in one of the local factories. "We didn't expect college," said Norris, none of whose siblings went to college, "but we didn't want to get our hands dirty in the mill."

Following the advice of one of Allen's navy buddies, the two had used the GI Bill to attend a school they knew nothing about, Princeton. Norris had gone on to Stanford Law School, clerked for Supreme Court Justice William O. Douglas and wound up a U.S. circuit court judge in Los Angeles. Allen had gone on to graduate work at Harvard and law school at Yale where he become a renowned expert on applying mathematical logic to legal problems. Almost certainly, neither man would have gone to college without the stimulus of the GI Bill. Even its supporters could scarcely have foreseen its boundless impact.

Aftermath

The GI Bill is still with us, though it has undergone a number of changes. The first peacetime version of the bill went into effect on the last day of 1972, after the draft officially ended, and was essentially a recruitment tool to lure recruits into the service after the disillusionment of the Vietnam War. The bill was renewed several times, until, in 1987, President Ronald Reagan signed a law designating it permanent and renaming it the "Montgomery GI Bill" in honor of Representative Sonny Montgomery of Mississippi, a veteran of World War II and the Korean conflict who, as chairman of the House Committee on Veterans Affairs, had worked on its behalf for years.

While many ex-GIs lined up to use the government's annual subsidy of $500 for college books and supplies (opposite page), others (top) stood in line to purchase one of the thousands of new houses (above) made possible by the GI Bill's provision guaranteeing home loans to returning veterans.

95

INDEX